All Things
MARSHMALLOW

All Things
MARSHMALLOW

Melt-in-the-mouth deliciousness
from The London Marshmallow Company

Ross O'Brien & Amy Nelson

jacqui
small

First published in 2015 by
Jacqui Small LLP
An imprint of Aurum Press
74–77 White Lion Street
London N1 9PF

Publisher: Jacqui Small
Senior Commissioning Editor: Fritha Saunders
Managing Editor: Emma Heyworth-Dunn
Senior Designer: Rachel Cross
Editor: Abi Waters
Production: Maeve Healy

ISBN: 978 1 910254 19 6

A catalogue record for this book is available from
the British Library.

2017 2016 2015
10 9 8 7 6 5 4 3 2 1

Printed in China

Contents

Why Marshmallows?

Everyone has eaten a marshmallow – from those spiralled, sugar-coated giant mallows, to the pink and white mini mallows sprinkled over whipped cream on your hot chocolate, or even the sticky mallow centre of a chocolate teacake. There is something a bit special about a marshmallow and there is nothing else quite like it. As a child, Amy remembers reading about homemade marshmallows in an old 1970s cookery book and not really believing that something so other-worldly could actually be made by hand and not just appear in packets in shops.

Marshmallows have a long history, originally a medicinal concoction extracted from the sap of the rather 'Willy Wonka' sounding marshmallow plant, *Althaea officinalis*. Marshmallow sweets were first eaten by the ancient Egyptians as a remedy for sore throats. We think you'll agree that their soothing, soft texture does sound rather appealing as an alternative to a lozenge! Many years later, in the 18th century, it was the French who combined the original marshmallow recipe with egg white to create *pâte de guimauve*.

It was this traditional French egg white recipe that we used when we finally took the plunge and first attempted to make marshmallows back in the winter of 2012. Despite putting it off for years, it was all suddenly so easy. A quick trip to the supermarket and armed with a sugar thermometer and a hand whisk (bad move, but more on that later), Ross, an excellent self-taught cook, made our very first batch… pillowy soft vanilla mallows – one bite and we were hooked!

We wanted to test the 'public's' reaction so a few weeks later after a meal of sliders and fries with friends at The Slaughtered Lamb in Farringdon, East London, we pulled out individual packets of vanilla and chocolate covered gingerbread mallows (flavours later to be known as The Angel and The Docklands). The delight and genuine surprise at such an original and delicious treat confirmed to us that we were on to something.

Next, it was time to see if anyone would part with their hard-earned cash for our mallows… so Ross took a batch to his work Christmas craft fair – we need not have worried, the little parcels were snapped up in minutes – and we made our first profit!

A few months later in April 2013 at Old Spitalfields Market we officially launched the The London Marshmallow Company with only had a handful of flavours to offer, including The Spitalfields – Lemon and Poppy Seed (see page 30). As the weeks went by, we slowly developed more and more flavours, naming each one after another place or part of our beloved city. This unique naming process has given each flavour an identity and customers love discovering the flavours of their favourite London destinations.

That long summer in 2013 was a blur of food markets and fashion and media events, plus our first wedding order. Finally, that November we settled down into a weekly routine of trading on a Saturday at Broadway in Hackney – one of the most exciting street food markets in London. It was from here we built our brand and gave The London Marshmallow Company regular exposure to the capital's foodies. Press features followed and with the wholesale and event side of the business booming, with heavy hearts we decided to stop trading at Broadway Market – exactly a year after we first started. That decision freed up some precious time as we had just been offered this opportunity to document our culinary delicacies in our very own book. The past few months have been a steady flow of recipe refinement, photoshoots and much typing! Seeing our book come to life has been the most rewarding part of our business so far and a fascinating creative journey. We hope you enjoy it as much as we have enjoyed creating it.

All Things Marshmallow covers both simple and complex marshmallow recipes but also shows you how marshmallows can be used in a whole variety of desserts, cakes, biscuits and treats. Marshmallows are the perfect vehicle for both classic and exotic flavour combinations. They are certainly a little bit naughty, but, being naturally low in fat, gluten free and handmade with the very best ingredients, they are an exquisite and grown-up way to enjoy a sweet treat. From taste to texture they are just so far removed from those pink and white mallows and yet still manage to conjure up fantastic childhood memories.

Read on to discover how to 'master the mallow' – a step-by-step guide to our basic marshmallow recipes needed throughout the book. Making marshmallows can be a little tricky but they certainly give the wow factor. As you gain confidence try our wide array of marshmallow recipes influenced by London's multicultural gastronomy. Learn how marshmallows can be both part of your weekly repertoire, served as the perfect homemade gift or even star as a centrepiece at a special event. The chapters that follow contain recipes suitable for all times of the year and all occasions, from surprising summer concoctions to traditional festive flavour combinations.

We hope *All Things Marshmallow* inspires you to make beautiful, natural mallows at home, for your friends and family to enjoy.

CHAPTER ONE

MASTER THE MALLOW

Mallow Basics

THE METHOD

The following step-by-step method illustrates the basic process for making the perfect marshmallow and the essential techniques involved. Always refer to individual recipes for exact measurements, ingredients, added flavourings and heating and mixing times.

Key points:

- It is important that your egg whites are whisked to stiff peaks (see step 1) so that you achieve a perfect, fluffy marshmallow.
- When you add the gelatine to the sugar syrup in step 3, the sugar will foam up a lot, so wait for the bubbles to die down before gently pouring in the remaining gelatine.
- If you are short on time, you can leave the marshmallows to set in the fridge for 2 hours rather than at room temperature. If you do this, make sure to return them to room temperature before turning out as this makes the mallow easier to cut.
- Make sure you clean the knife and reapply the dusting as you cut, as it will quickly become too sticky to use effectively.
- Marshmallows do not need to be kept in the fridge – they are best eaten as fresh as possible but can be stored in an airtight container at room temperature for 2 weeks or frozen for 4 weeks (see page 156).

1. Whisking egg whites
Whisk the required quantity of egg whites to stiff peaks using an electric stand mixer. They should be firm enough to hold their peaks when you lift the whisk out of the bowl.

2. Dissolving gelatine
Pour boiling water into a bowl, evenly sprinkle over powdered gelatine and gently stir in with a whisk until fully dissolved.

3. Making sugar syrup
Put the required sugar, golden syrup and water in a heavy-based pan and set over a high heat for 10 minutes, or until it reaches either 113°C/235°F (soft-ball stage) or 127°C/260°F (hard-ball stage) on a sugar thermometer as instructed in the recipe. Turn off the heat, pour in 2 tablespoons of the gelatine and stir. Pour in the remaining gelatine.

4. Adding sugar syrup to egg whites
Once all the bubbles have dissipated, turn the mixer to a medium speed and slowly pour the sugar mix into the egg whites. Turn up to full speed – it will loosen and turn glossy. Keep mixing for as long as instructed until it has doubled in size and is the same consistency as lightly whipped cream.

5. Pouring into the tin

Pour the mallow into a baking tin lightly sprayed with cake-release spray. Spread out evenly, cover with cling film and set aside overnight or for 8 hours at room temperature to firm up.

6. Turning out

Carefully remove the cling film. Use a 50:50 mixture of cornflour and icing sugar to dust the top of the mallow and the work surface. Gently turn out and dust the top of the mallow.

7. Dusting

Dust a large knife and the surface of the marshmallow with the cornflour/icing sugar mix – marshmallows are incredibly sticky!

8. Cutting lengthways

Starting in the middle, cut the mallow into 6 even, long pieces.

9. Final cuts

Cut each of these long pieces into 6 again, giving 36 square mallows. Clean the knife and reapply the dusting as you work.

10. Coating the mallows

Gently roll all the marshmallows in the cornflour/icing sugar mix to finish.

EQUIPMENT

You should already have in your kitchen almost all equipment used in marshmallow making.

- **Electric stand mixer** – the timings in this book are based on using a stand mixer. You can use a handheld electric whisk but you will get a very achy arm as we found out when we made our very first batch!
- **Sugar thermometer** – this is a must and can be purchased online or in cookery shops.
- **Silicone spatula** – silicone is suitable for very high temperatures and essential for scraping every last drop of mixture out of jugs and bowls.
- **Small and large heavy-based saucepans**
- **Pyrex jug and spoon measures**
- **Digital scales**
- **Large sharp knife** – at least 23cm (9 inches) long.
- **Balloon whisk**
- **Handheld electric whisk** – needed for a few recipes (Marshmallow Crème, page 17) so is useful to have.
- **23 x 23cm (9 x 9 inch) square baking tin** – a larger tin can be used but will create a flatter mallow.
- **Kitchen blowtorch** – useful for bruléeing frosting.

INGREDIENTS

Most ingredients needed can be purchased from any large supermarket – for anything slightly unusual or technical please see our Useful Information section on page 156.

- **White caster/granulated sugar**
  We recommend white caster or granulated sugar – it doesn't matter which type as it will all be melted down in the recipe.
- **Powdered gelatine**
  Our recipes use powdered gelatine as we find it easier to adjust the amount required for different recipes. See page 156 for an alternative setting agent.
- **Free-range egg whites**
  Always use fresh free-range egg whites and check the size required in each recipe. The amount used will vary and too much will create a mallow that is too fluffy.
- **Golden syrup**
  This is an essential ingredient in all mallow recipes as it prevents the sugar from recrystallizing as it cools.
- **Water**
  Boiling water and cold water are needed in most of our recipes. The boiling water is required to dissolve the gelatine, then the cold water is used to make the sugar syrup.
- **Fruit, nuts, extracts and spices**
  To flavour the marshmallows, we use real fruit (in the form of purées and freeze-dried powders), plus nuts, spices, alcohol and natural extracts.

Mallow Q&A

Here we have tried to answer any potential questions you might have while making marshmallows. There are so many variables with mallow making – temperatures, volumes and brands used – so it may be that you need to get creative and experiment if something doesn't quite work the first time.

Can I use unrefined sugar?
We wouldn't recommend using an unrefined sugar as it will create an off-white colour and a stickier mallow.

Can I use leaf gelatine?
Powdered and leaf gelatine have different setting strengths. It is possible to use leaf gelatine instead of powdered, but you may need to test it out and tweak the amounts slightly.

Can I use extra sugar instead of golden syrup?
No – if extra sugar is used instead the sugar will recrystallize as it cools, which will result in a grainy texture.

If I can't get hold of golden syrup what can I use?
Liquid glucose can be used as an alternative.

What size egg whites do you use?
We use both medium free-range egg whites (about 35g/1¼oz each) and large free-range egg whites (about 40g/1½oz each).

Are egg whites safe to eat?
If at all concerned about eating egg whites, use pasteurized liquid egg whites. If using whole eggs, use fresh Lion Quality stamped eggs.

Why are my marshmallows not set properly and too soft?
The three main reasons for this would be:

◆ Not enough gelatine – try increasing the amount as each brand is different. The recipes in this book are based on supermarket baking brand Dr. Oetker powdered gelatine.

◆ Too much liquid – try reducing the water, purée or juice added after the sugar syrup has come to temperature.

◆ Too much egg white – try reducing the egg white. Egg white gives the mallow its fluffy texture but too much and it will be too fluffy.

Madagascan Vanilla Marshmallow

**MAKES 36 LARGE
MARSHMALLOWS**

2 large egg whites
150ml (5fl oz) boiling water
30g (1⅛oz) powdered gelatine
500g (1lb 2oz) white granulated
  or caster sugar
4 teaspoons golden syrup
200ml (7fl oz) cold water
1 teaspoon Madagascan vanilla
  bean paste
Cornflour and icing sugar,
  for dusting

23 x 23cm (9 x 9 inch) baking
  tin lightly sprayed with cake-
  release spray

Our signature vanilla egg white mallow forms the basis for many of our other marshmallows and is a key recipe for any budding marshmallow-maker to master. These gentle, subtly flavoured mallows can be eaten as they are or added to desserts or hot drinks.

1. Whisk the egg whites to stiff peaks using an electric stand mixer and set aside. Pour the boiling water into a bowl, evenly sprinkle over the gelatine and gently whisk until fully dissolved.

2. Use the sugar, golden syrup and cold water to make a hard-ball sugar syrup, add the gelatine and combine with the egg whites as described on page 10. Keep mixing on full speed for 10 minutes until the mixture is the same consistency as lightly whipped double cream. For the last 30 seconds of mixing, add the vanilla paste and mix in.

3. Turn off the mixer and pour the mallow into the baking tin. Make sure it is evenly spread out, then cover with cling film. Leave to set as described on page 11.

4. Turn out and cut the mallow as described on page 11.

5. Enjoy these mallows straightaway or keep them in an airtight container for 2 weeks.

Egg-free Variation

Use the same ingredients as above, except for the egg white, and proceed as follows.

1. Pour the boiling water into the stand mixer bowl, evenly sprinkle over the powdered gelatine and gently whisk with a hand balloon whisk until fully dissolved.

2. Use the sugar, golden syrup and water to make a hard-ball sugar syrup as described on page 10. After about 5 minutes, start whisking the gelatine mixture in the stand mixer on high speed until frothy and doubled in volume.

3. Once the sugar has come to temperature, slowly add it to the frothy gelatine and keep mixing for 5 minutes until the mixture is the same consistency as lightly whipped double cream. For the last 30 seconds of mixing, add the vanilla paste.

4. Continue with the method as above from step 3.

Marshmallow Crème

**MAKES A 180G (6OZ) JAR
OF CRÈME**

150g (5½oz) white granulated
   or caster sugar
3 medium egg whites
30g (1⅛oz) golden syrup

Marshmallow crème is a soft fluffy alternative to normal marshmallow.
It can be spooned liberally onto pancakes, waffles or hot chocolate
and later in the book you will see how we also use it to create
toppings and fillings for many other treats.

1. Set a large heatproof bowl over a saucepan of just simmering water, making sure
the water is not touching the base of the bowl. Add all the ingredients and whisk with
a handheld electric whisk for 12–14 minutes.

2. Once the mixture forms stiff, glossy peaks, transfer to a sterile jar or bowl and cover
the mallow surface with cling film or parchment to prevent a skin from forming. The
crème can be enjoyed straightaway or kept in the jar in the fridge for 3 days.

Marshmallow Fluff

**MAKES A 180G (6OZ) JAR
OF FLUFF**

1 medium egg white
50ml (2fl oz) boiling water
12g (½oz) powdered gelatine
135g (4¾oz) white granulated
   or caster sugar
15g (½oz) golden syrup
50ml (2fl oz) cold water

Unlike the crème, this contains gelatine and will set firm but fluffy. We
use it to create the filling for biscuits and brownies later in the book.

1. Whisk the egg white to stiff peaks using an electric stand mixer and set aside. Pour
the boiling water into a bowl, evenly sprinkle over the powdered gelatine and gently
whisk until fully dissolved.

2. Use the sugar, golden syrup and cold water to make a soft-ball sugar syrup, add the
gelatine and combine with the egg white until it turns glossy as described on page 10.
Keep mixing on full speed for 6–7 minutes until the mixture is the same consistency
as lightly whipped double cream.

3. Once made, transfer the soft mallow to a piping bag and use immediately.

Homemade Nut Praline

**MAKES 100G (3½OZ) –
ENOUGH FOR ABOUT 2 TINS
OF MARSHMALLOWS**

40g (1½oz) white granulated sugar
60g (2oz) unsalted raw nuts of your
   choice, roughly chopped
Good pinch of Maldon sea salt

Nut praline is super easy to make and can be roughly chopped up to add to a variety of the recipes coming up. It's also great on top of ice cream or other desserts – up the salt if you really love that sweet and salty taste sensation!

1. Pour the sugar into a saucepan in an even layer and set over a medium to high temperature. Heat the sugar, gently moving the pan in a circular motion to help the sugar melt evenly. Continue until the sugar is a rusty brown colour, starts to smoke and small bubbles appear.

2. Quickly take the pan off the heat and add the chopped nuts. Work quickly to mix the caramel and nuts together until they are all coated.

3. Spoon the hot sticky praline out of the pan onto a non-stick baking tray and sprinkle over a good pinch of sea salt.

4. Once the praline is cool and hard (this will take about 30 minutes) remove from the baking tray and chop up with a sharp knife.

5. The praline is now ready to add to marshmallow mixtures as required or to sprinkle over desserts and ice cream. It can be stored for up to 6 weeks in a good airtight container.

Homemade Fruit Purée

MAKES ABOUT 250G (9OZ)

350g (12oz) of your chosen fruit

We use fruit purée to make lots of different fruit mallows – unlike fruit compote, fruit purée is not cooked and no sugar needs to be added.

1. Carefully wash the fruit under a cold tap. If the fruit has a skin, such as apples and pears, peel and core the fruit. Soft fruits (like peaches and apricots) need to be blanched in boiling water first for 45 seconds before peeling and removing the stones.

2. Add the fruit to a food processor and blend until smooth (you may need to push the fruit down with a spoon every now and again and use the 'pulse' button).

3. If the fruit had thin skins you couldn't peel or tiny seeds (like blueberries and raspberries) you may want to push the purée through a fine sieve to get the mixture extra smooth.

4. The fruit purée can now be used in many of the fruit marshmallow recipes found in this book. Store in an airtight container in the fridge for 2 days.

CHAPTER TWO

SUMMER FAVOURITES

Strawberry and Vanilla Mallows

MAKES 36 LARGE MARSHMALLOWS

For the vanilla layer

1 large egg white
75ml (2¾fl oz) boiling water
15g (½oz) powdered gelatine
250g (9oz) white granulated or caster sugar
2 teaspoons golden syrup
100ml (3½fl oz) cold water
½ teaspoon Madagascan vanilla bean paste

For the strawberry layer

1 large egg white
150ml (5fl oz) cold water
20g (¾oz) freeze-dried strawberry powder
70ml (3fl oz) boiling water
18g (¾oz) powdered gelatine
250g (9½oz) white granulated or caster sugar
2 teaspoons golden syrup
½ teaspoon natural pink food colouring

To finish

Cornflour and icing sugar, for dusting
100g (3½oz) white chocolate, finely chopped
18 small fresh strawberries, halved

23 x 23cm (9 x 9 inch) baking tin lightly sprayed with cake-release spray

What could be more summery? Reminiscent of the classic combination of strawberries and cream, this layered marshmallow looks stunning topped with white chocolate and strawberry halves.

1. To make the vanilla layer, use the ingredients to make a half batch of Madagascan Vanilla Marshmallows as described on page 14 – you will need to reduce the heating and mixing times by half as well. Once the vanilla layer is in the tin and covered with cling film, start the next layer straightaway.

2. To make the strawberry layer, whisk the egg white to stiff peaks using an electric stand mixer and set aside. Add 50ml (2fl oz) of the cold water to the strawberry powder, thoroughly stir and set aside. Pour the boiling water into a bowl, evenly sprinkle over the gelatine and gently whisk until fully dissolved.

3. Use the sugar, golden syrup and remaining cold water to make a hard-ball sugar syrup, add the gelatine and combine with the egg white until it turns glossy as described on page 10. Keep mixing on full speed for 3 minutes, stop the mixer and add the strawberry mixture. Turn the mixer back on to full speed for a further 2 minutes until the mixture has the same consistency as lightly whipped double cream. Add the pink colouring for the last 30 seconds of mixing until fully combined.

4. Remove the cling film from the vanilla mallow. Pour the strawberry mallow on top of the vanilla layer, making sure it is evenly spread, then cover with cling film. Leave to set as described on page 11.

5. Turn out and cut the mallow as described on page 11.

6. Now you're ready to decorate. Put about 1 litre (35fl oz) of boiling water in a large saucepan. Place a large heatproof bowl over the pan to act as a lid and a vessel that the chocolate will melt in – make sure the base of the bowl is not touching the water. Bring the water up to a steady simmer, then turn off the heat. Put the chopped chocolate in the bowl and leave for 5–10 minutes, stirring occasionally, allowing the residual heat to melt the chocolate.

7. Use a teaspoon to create a small disc of white chocolate on the top surface of each mallow and top with a strawberry half. Enjoy these mallows straightaway or store in an airtight container for a couple of days.

Mini Summer Cupcakes

These mini cupcakes have all the makings of a glass of Pimm's – the sponge is infused with Pimm's liqueur and fresh orange zest and the strawberry marshmallow buttercrème frosting is topped with a slice of fresh strawberry, cucumber and a sprig of fresh mint.

MAKES 20 MINI CUPCAKES

125g (4¼oz) unsalted butter, softened
150g (5½oz) golden caster sugar
Grated zest of 1 orange
3 large eggs, beaten
50ml (2fl oz) Pimm's
150g (5½oz) self-raising flour

For the Pimm's syrup
150ml (5fl oz) Pimm's
Juice of 1 orange
50g (1¾oz) white granulated or caster sugar

For the marshmallow buttercrème topping
1 quantity of Marshmallow Crème (see page 17)
150g (5½oz) unsalted butter, softened
100g (3½oz) icing sugar
15g (½oz) freeze-dried strawberry powder

To decorate
Fresh strawberries, sliced
Cucumber slices
Fresh mint sprigs

20-hole mini cupcake tin and mini cupcake cases
Piping bag fitted with a wide nozzle

1. Preheat the oven to 200°C/180°C fan/400°F/Gas Mark 6. Line the cupcake tin with cupcake cases.

2. Using an electric stand mixer, cream together the butter, sugar and orange zest until light and fluffy. Combine the eggs and Pimm's in a separate bowl, then slowly add this mixture to the creamed butter and sugar. Add the flour a tablespoon at a time until fully combined.

3. Spoon the mixture into the 20 mini cupcake cases and bake for 10–12 minutes.

4. While the cupcakes are baking, make the Pimm's syrup. Place the Pimm's, orange juice and sugar in a small saucepan and boil for about 8 minutes until reduced by two-thirds, to form a light syrup.

5. When the cupcakes are golden on top and spring back when lightly pressed with a finger, remove them from the oven and prick each one 3–4 times with a skewer. Place the cupcakes on a wire rack and spoon a small amount of syrup onto each one.

6. Make the Marshmallow Crème (see page 17), cover and set aside. Cream together the butter and icing sugar until smooth and fluffy to form a buttercream. Add the buttercream to the Marshmallow Crème a tablespoon at a time, beating in fully after each addition of buttercream, adding the strawberry powder at the end.

7. Spoon the strawberry marshmallow buttercrème into a piping bag fitted with a wide nozzle. Carefully pipe a swirl of the buttercrème on top of each cupcake and top with a slice of fresh strawberry, cucumber and sprig of fresh mint.

Toasted Coconut Marshmallows

MAKES 36 LARGE MARSHMALLOWS

2 large egg whites
150ml (5fl oz) boiling water
30g (1⅛oz) powdered gelatine
500g (1lb 2oz) white granulated or caster sugar
4 teaspoons golden syrup
200ml (7fl oz) cold water
50g (1¾oz) organic desiccated coconut
25g (1oz) toasted flaked coconut, chopped (optional)
Cornflour and icing sugar, for dusting

23 x 23cm (9 x 9 inch) baking tin lightly sprayed with cake-release spray

Simple classic coconut marshmallows – we often make these pale blue for weddings or they can be left snowy white. These are great in a hot chocolate with a slug of coconut liqueur.

1. Whisk the egg whites to stiff peaks using an electric stand mixer and set aside. Pour the boiling water into a bowl, evenly sprinkle over the powdered gelatine and gently whisk until fully dissolved.

2. Use the sugar, golden syrup and water to make a hard-ball sugar syrup, add the gelatine and combine with the egg whites until they turn glossy as described on page 10. Keep mixing on full speed for 10 minutes until the mixture is the same consistency as lightly whipped double cream. Turn off the mixer and gently stir in the coconut with a spatula.

3. Pour the marshmallow into the baking tin. Make sure it is evenly spread out and scatter with the flaked coconut, if using. Cover with cling film and leave to set as described on page 11.

4. Turn out and cut the mallow as described on page 11.

5. Enjoy these mallows straightaway or keep in an airtight container for 2 weeks.

Flavour variation Layered Raspberry and Coconut Marshmallows

Turn this into a fantastic layered marshmallow by making a half batch of the coconut marshmallows as above, halving the ingredients, heating and mixing times. Pour into the prepared tin and cover with cling film while you make the raspberry layer from the Strawberry and Vanilla Mallows (see page 22), substituting the strawberry powder with freeze-fried raspberry powder. Pour this on top of the coconut layer and scatter the surface with 1 teaspoon freeze-dried raspberry powder and 25g (1oz) chopped toasted flaked coconut. Cover with cling film, leave to set, then continue with steps 4 and 5 above.

Passion Fruit and Mango Marshmallow Eton Mess

SERVES 6

6 large Passion Fruit and Mango
  Marshmallows *(see page 36)*
12 mini meringues *(see page 60)*
  – or you could use 3 shop-bought
  meringue nests, about 8cm
  (3¼ inch) diameter
1 large mango, cubed
500ml (14fl oz) whipping cream,
  whipped
Flesh and seeds of 3 passion fruit
Handful of Candied Chillies *(see
  page 36)*

This marshmallow Eton mess can be made with any of our fruit marshmallows – try the Lemon and Blueberry Marshmallow (see page 31) and combine with fresh blueberries, lemon curd and lemon zest; or use blackcurrants and blackberries with the Layered Elderflower and Blackcurrant Marshmallows (see page 74) and top with fresh elderflower blossoms.

1. Cut the marshmallows into eighths and break the meringues into large chunks.

2. Gently fold the cubes of mango, whipped cream, marshmallow pieces and broken meringues together in a large bowl.

3. Divide the mixture between 6 dessert bowls, top with a spoonful of the passion fruit seeds and juice and scatter with some candied chillies to finish.

Lemon and Poppy Seed Marshmallows

MAKES 36 LARGE MARSHMALLOWS

2 medium egg whites
90ml (3fl oz) boiling water
36g (1¼oz) powdered gelatine
500g (1lb 2oz) white granulated or caster sugar
4 teaspoons golden syrup
200ml (7fl oz) cold water
120ml (4fl oz) fresh lemon juice (about 3 large lemons)
1 teaspoon lemon extract
1 teaspoon natural yellow food colouring
1 tablespoon poppy seeds
Grated zest of 3 lemons
Cornflour and icing sugar, to dust

23 x 23cm (9 x 9 inch) baking tin lightly sprayed with cake-release spray

Lemon marshmallows were one of the first flavours we developed when we started the business. We called it The Spitalfields in honour of the first market we traded at in London – Old Spitalfields. Originally a fruit market, the Spitalfields area in East London was also once renowned for its opium dens so using poppy seeds feels like a nod to the social history of the area.

1. Whisk the egg whites to stiff peaks using an electric stand mixer and set aside. Pour the boiling water into a bowl, evenly sprinkle over the powdered gelatine and gently whisk until fully dissolved.

2. Use the sugar, golden syrup and cold water to make a hard-ball sugar syrup, add the gelatine and combine with the egg whites until they turn glossy as described on page 10. Keep mixing on full speed for 10 minutes until the mixture is the same consistency as lightly whipped double cream. Add the lemon extract and yellow colouring and mix for a further 30 seconds until completely mixed in.

3. Turn off the mixer and pour the marshmallow into the baking tin. Make sure it is evenly spread out, then scatter the surface with the poppy seeds and lemon zest. Cover with cling film and leave to set as described on page 11.

4. Turn out and cut the mallow as described on page 11.

5. Enjoy these mallows straightaway or keep in an airtight container for 2 weeks.

Flavour variation

Layered Lemon and Blueberry Marshmallows

Turn this into a fantastic layered marshmallow by making a half batch of the Lychee and Lime Marshmallows (see page 34), but replace the lychee purée with 100ml (3½fl oz) blueberry purée and omit the lime; remember to halve the other ingredients and the heating and mixing times. Pour into a prepared tin and make a half batch of the lemon marshmallows as opposite, halving the ingredients, heating and mixing times. Pour on top of the blueberry layer. Scatter the surface with the grated zest of 2 lemons, cover with cling film, then continue with the recipe opposite.

Lemon Curd Tart with Bruléed Mallow Topping

SERVES 10

For the crust

85g (3oz) Hobnob biscuits, crushed
75g (2¾oz) unsalted butter, melted
65g (2¼oz) plain flour
65g (2¼oz) organic desiccated
   coconut
1 tablespoon caster sugar

For the lemon curd

5 medium egg yolks (retain 1 egg
   white)
300ml (10½oz) sweetened
   condensed milk
Juice of 3-4 lemons (about ⅔cup)
1 tablespoon grated lemon zest

For the marshmallow layer

1 quantity of Marshmallow Fluff
   (see page 17)

20cm (8 inch) round springform
   cake tin sprayed with cake-release
   spray and lined with greaseproof
   paper
Piping bag fitted with a wide nozzle
Blowtorch

This cheesecake-lemon meringue pie hybrid is a great dessert after a summer Sunday lunch, with its sweet bruléed marshmallow topping that contrasts with the sharp lemon curd layer.

1. Preheat the oven to 200°C/180°C fan/400°F/Gas Mark 6. First, make the tart crust. Combine the crust ingredients in a mixing bowl, then press it into the bottom of the prepared tin in an even layer. Bake the crust for 12 minutes, remove from the oven and leave to cool. Turn the oven down to 170°C/150°C fan/325°F/Gas mark 3.

2. Next, make the lemon curd. Whisk all the ingredients, except the lemon zest, in a bowl until smooth. Stir in the lemon zest. Pour the lemon curd over the baked crust and bake for 20–25 minutes until just set. Remove from the oven and leave to cool. Once cool, chill in the fridge for 1 hour.

3. For the marshmallow layer, make the Marshmallow Fluff as described on page 17. Spoon the soft mallow into a piping bag fitted with wide nozzle and pipe over the set, chilled lemon curd layer. Use the back of a spoon or a palette knife to create a smooth surface.

4. Put the pie back in the fridge for 1 hour until the marshmallow is set. Remove from the fridge and release from the tin onto a serving plate. When ready to serve, use a kitchen blowtorch to lightly brulée the marshmallow layer before slicing into portions.

Lychee and Lime Mallows
with a Cashew Nut Crumb

**MAKES 36 LARGE
MARSHMALLOWS**

2 medium egg whites
90ml (3fl oz) boiling water
36g (1¼oz) powdered gelatine
500g (1lb 2 oz) white granulated
 or caster sugar
4 teaspoons golden syrup
300ml (10fl oz) lychee purée
 or juice
Grated zest and juice of 1 lime
½ teaspoon natural pink food
 colouring
30g (1⅛oz) chopped salted toasted
 cashew nuts
Cornflour and icing sugar, for
 dusting

23 x 23cm (9 x 9 inch) baking
 tin lightly sprayed with cake-
 release spray

Lychee is a delicate flavour so we give this mallow extra 'zing' with fresh lime juice and zest plus we top with chopped salted cashew nuts for extra texture – macadamia or brazil nuts would also work well.

1. Whisk the egg whites to stiff peaks using an electric stand mixer and set aside. Pour the boiling water into a bowl, evenly sprinkle over the powdered gelatine and gently whisk until fully dissolved.

2. Use the sugar, golden syrup and 200ml (7fl oz) of the lychee purée or juice to make a hard-ball sugar syrup, add the gelatine and combine with the egg whites until they turn glossy as described on page 10. Keep mixing on full speed for 5 minutes, then stop the mixer and add the remaining lychee purée or juice and the lime juice. Turn the mixer back on to full speed for another 5 minutes until the mixture is the same consistency as lightly whipped double cream. Add the pink colouring and mix for a further 30 seconds until completely mixed in.

3. Turn off the mixer and pour the marshmallow into the baking tin. Make sure it is evenly spread out, then scatter the surface with the chopped cashews and lime zest. Cover with cling film and leave to set as described on page 11.

4. Turn out and cut the mallow as described on page 11.

5. Enjoy these mallows straightaway or keep in an airtight container for 2 weeks.

Tropical Fruit and Lychee Marshmallow Skewers

**MAKES 12 SKEWERS
(SERVES 4)**

6 Lychee and Lime Mallows *(see
page 34)*, cut diagonally in half
½ pineapple, peeled and cut into
chunks
3 persimmons, peeled and cut into
chunks
4 kiwi fruit, peeled and cut into
chunks
100g (3½oz) dark chocolate, broken
into pieces
Handful of toasted coconut

Bamboo or wooden skewers
Piping bag for chocolate (optional)

These skewers are great for a summer barbecue or pool party – they
can be prepared in advance and chilled or can be made by guests as
and when they want them.

1. Thread a mixture of fruit and marshmallow chunks onto each skewer, then lay them
out flat on a large tray.

2. Melt the chocolate as described on page 22 (step 6) and spoon it into a piping bag
with a narrow nozzle, if using. Carefully pipe or drizzle the skewers with the dark
chocolate and scatter over the toasted coconut.

3. Transfer the tray to the fridge for the chocolate to set, then arrange on a large platter
when ready to serve.

Tip: The fruit can be exchanged for whatever fruit or berries
you prefer, such as mango, banana,
strawberries or papaya.

Passion Fruit and Mango Marshmallows
Topped with Candied Red Chillies

**MAKES 36 LARGE
MARSHMALLOWS**

2 medium egg whites
90ml (3fl oz) boiling water
36g (1¼oz) powdered gelatine
¼ teaspoon chilli powder
250g (9oz) white granulated or
    caster sugar
250ml (8½fl oz) chilli sugar syrup
    (leftover from making the candied
    chillies – see Tip)
4 teaspoons golden syrup
125ml (4¼fl oz) mango purée
125ml (4¼fl oz) passion fruit purée
Cornflour and icing sugar, for
    dusting

For the candied chillies
250g (9oz) white granulated sugar
250ml (8½fl oz) cold water
3 medium-hot red chillies, washed,
    deseeded and finely sliced

23 x 23cm (9 x 9 inch) baking
    tin lightly sprayed with cake-
    release spray

This marshmallow packs quite a punch! The candied red chillies can be pretty hot but they complement the sweet mango and passion fruit marshmallow perfectly.

1. First, make the Candied Chillies. Preheat the oven to 110°C/90°C fan/195°F/Gas Mark ¼. Heat the sugar and water in a heavy-based saucepan over a high heat until completely dissolved, then add the sliced chillies. Turn the heat down to a simmer and poach the chillies in the syrup for 30 minutes. Strain the syrup using a sieve (reserving the syrup for the marshmallow recipe below) and place the chillies on a clean baking sheet and dry in the oven for 1 hour. Remove the chillies and once cool, chop into finer pieces. (The chillies will keep in an airtight jar for 3 months.)

2. Next, make the marshmallow. Whisk the egg whites to stiff peaks using an electric stand mixer and set aside. Pour the boiling water into a bowl, evenly sprinkle over the powdered gelatine and chilli powder and gently whisk until fully dissolved.

3. Use the sugar, golden syrup, chilli sugar syrup and 75ml (2½fl oz) each of the mango and passion fruit purées to make a hard-ball sugar syrup, add the gelatine and combine with the egg whites until they turn glossy as described on page 10. Keep mixing on full speed for 5 minutes, stop the mixer and add the remaining mango and passion fruit purées. Turn the mixer back on to full speed for another 5 minutes until the mixture is the same consistency as lightly whipped double cream.

4. Turn off the mixer and pour the marshmallow from the bowl into the prepared baking tin. Make sure it is evenly spread out, then scatter the surface with the candied chillies. Cover with cling film and leave to set as described on page 11.

5. Turn out and cut the mallow as described on page 11.

6. Enjoy these mallows straightaway or keep in an airtight container for 2 weeks.

Tip: Using the syrup from making the candied chillies packs an extra punch in the mallow mix however you can just use another 250g (9oz) granulated sugar instead.

Citrus Marshmallow Mousse Cups
with Macerated Raspberries

SERVES 6

600ml (1 pint) double cream
150ml (5fl oz) milk
Grated zest and juice of 1 lime
14 Lemon and Poppy Seed
  Marshmallows *(see page 30),* cut
  into halves (cut the tops off the
  mallows if you would rather not
  have the poppy seeds visible here)
450g (1lb) fresh or defrosted
  raspberries
1 tablespoon icing sugar

This decadent dessert is super easy to make. We top this sweet lemon mousse-style dessert with a simple spoonful of macerated raspberries.

1. Bring the cream and milk to the boil in a heavy-based saucepan, stirring occasionally. Add the lime zest and juice, stirring for a further minute while still on the heat, until the mixture thickens slightly.

2. Take the pan off the heat, add the marshmallows and stir until the mallows have fully melted.

3. Pass the mixture through a sieve into a jug to remove the larger pieces of zest. Pour the mixture evenly into 6 cups or glasses. Once at room temperature, cover with cling film and chill in the fridge for 8 hours until set.

4. About 10 minutes before serving, wash the raspberries and place them in a large bowl. Dust the raspberries with the icing sugar and leave in the bowl until they start to break up and macerate.

5. When ready to serve, place the cups or glasses onto plates and top with a large spoonful of the macerated raspberries.

Tip: Other flavour marshmallows (such as strawberry and vanilla or mango and passion fruit) can easily be substituted.

Almond and Vanilla Whoopee Pies

MAKES 40

225g (8oz) plain flour
50g (1¾oz) ground almonds
¾ teaspoon bicarbonate of soda
½ teaspoon salt
1 medium egg
150g (5½oz) caster sugar
75g (2¾oz) unsalted butter, melted
150ml (5fl oz) buttermilk
1 teaspoon almond extract
Sugar-coated mini chocolate eggs
  and/or flaked almonds

**For the vanilla marshmallow
  buttercrème**
1 quantity of Marshmallow Crème
  (see page 17)
150g (5½oz) unsalted butter
100g (3½oz) icing sugar
1 teaspoon vanilla bean paste

Piping bag fitted with a wide nozzle

These mini whoopee pies are so pretty – the mini eggs make them the perfect little treat for Easter but they can easily be left plain with the crunchy toasted flaked almond topping – fantastic served with coffee!

1. Preheat the oven to 200°C/180°C fan/400°F/Gas Mark 6. Line two large baking trays with greaseproof paper. Sift the flour, ground almonds, bicarbonate of soda and salt together into a medium bowl and set aside.

2. Whisk the egg and sugar together for 3–4 minutes using an electric stand mixer until light and fluffy. Add the melted butter, buttermilk and almond extract and whisk until combined. Fold in the sifted flour mixture.

3. Spoon a teaspoonful of the dough for each cookie onto the baking trays. They need to be spaced about 3cm (1 inch) apart so you should fit about 40 onto each baking tray. For an added flourish, you could sprinkle the raw cookies with flaked almonds before baking for a crunchy topping. Bake for 6–7 minutes or until the cookies spring back when lightly touched. Transfer the baking trays to wire racks and leave to cool.

4. To make the vanilla marshmallow buttercrème, make the Marshmallow Crème (see page 17), cover and set aside. Cream together the butter and icing sugar until smooth and fluffy to form a buttercream. Add the buttercream to the marshmallow crème a tablespoon at a time, beating in fully after each addition of buttercream. Once smooth and fluffy, add the vanilla paste and mix until completely combined.

5. Transfer the vanilla marshmallow buttercrème to a piping bag fitted with a wide nozzle. Assemble the whoopee pies by piping filling onto the flat side of one cookie and topping with another. To decorate, pipe a small dot of buttercrème on top of each cookie and then place a sugar-coated mini egg on top of this.

Prosecco and Rosemary Poached Peach Sundae

This simple dessert of poached peaches is delicious made into a modern sundae served with good-quality vanilla ice cream and our Peach and Prosecco Marshmallows (see opposite). The fresh rosemary adds an unexpected savoury note.

SERVES 6

100g (3½ oz) caster sugar
500ml (18fl oz) prosecco
15ml (1 tablespoon) Amaretto liqueur
4 large ripe peaches or nectarines, halved and stoned
Large sprig of rosemary, plus extra sprig to finish
3–6 large Peach and Prosecco Marshmallows (*see page 43*), chopped into smaller pieces
Good-quality vanilla ice cream

1. Put the sugar, prosecco and Amaretto in a heavy-based saucepan and bring to a gentle simmer.

2. Score 2 lines on the skin of each peach half, running from base to top, and place them in the saucepan – if the peaches are not fully submerged top up with a little water.

3. Lightly simmer the peaches in the syrup for 5–10 minutes until tender but not overly soft. Remove the peaches from the pan with a slotted spoon and set aside to cool.

4. Add the rosemary to the syrup, increase the heat and reduce the syrup by about two-thirds. This will take about 10 minutes.

5. Once the peaches are cool, peel and slice them.

6. When ready to serve, distribute the sliced peaches between 6 champagne saucers or glass dishes. Add a small handful of the chopped marshmallows to each dish and spoon the pink syrup over each bowl. Add a scoop of vanilla ice cream and top with a few rosemary leaves. Serve immediately and enjoy!

Peach and Prosecco Marshmallows

**MAKES 36 LARGE
MARSHMALLOWS**

2 medium egg whites

150ml (5fl oz) prosecco

36g (1¼ oz) powdered gelatine

500g (1lb 2oz) white granulated
sugar

4 teaspoons golden syrup

50ml (2fl oz) cold water

225g (8oz) white peach purée (see
page 19)

Edible gold leaf (about 9 pieces),
to decorate

Cornflour and icing sugar, for
dusting

23 x 23cm (9 x 9 inch) baking
tin lightly sprayed with cake-
release spray

We use white peach purée and real Italian prosecco in these
marshmallows, which are reminiscent of a classic Bellini cocktail.
Topped with real edible gold leaf they are truly decadent.

1. Whisk the egg whites to stiff peaks using an electric stand mixer and set aside.
Warm 100ml (3½fl oz) of the prosecco in a saucepan, evenly sprinkle over the
powdered gelatine and stir until dissolved.

2. Use the sugar, golden syrup, cold water and 150ml (5fl oz) of the peach purée to
make a hard-ball sugar syrup, add the gelatine and combine with the egg whites until
they turn glossy as described on page 10. Keep mixing on full speed for 5 minutes,
stop the mixer and add the remaining peach purée and prosecco. Turn the mixer back
on to full speed for another 5 minutes until the mixture is the same consistency as
lightly whipped double cream.

3. Turn off the mixer and pour the marshmallow from the bowl into the prepared
baking tin. Cover with cling film and leave to set as described on page 11.

4. Once firm, but before cutting, add gold leaf to the top sticky surface of the
marshmallow. Turn out and cut the mallow as described on page 11. Enjoy these
mallows straightaway or keep in an airtight container for 2 weeks.

Raspberry Ombre Celebration Cake

MAKES ONE LARGE CAKE (SERVES 16)

300g (10½oz) unsalted butter, softened
300g (10½oz) caster sugar
6 large eggs, beaten
300g (10½oz) self-raising flour
1½ teaspoons baking powder
2½ tablespoons milk
½ teaspoon salt

For the marshmallow crème topping

2 quantities of Marshmallow Crème (see page 17)
300g (10½oz) unsalted butter, softened
200g (7oz) icing sugar
½ teaspoon vanilla bean paste
15g (¾oz) freeze-dried raspberry powder

For the filling

200g (7oz) raspberry jam
500g (1lb 2oz) raspberries

Three 20cm (8 inch) springform cake tins lightly sprayed with cake-release spray
3 piping bags fitted with wide nozzles

This cake looks stunning and tastes amazing, too. Fresh raspberries bleed into the sponge creating a moist cake with a tart raspberry flavour that contrasts perfectly with the light, sugary marshmallow buttercrème icing.

1. Preheat the oven to 210°C/190°C fan/415°F/Gas Mark 5–6. Line the greased cake tins with greaseproof paper and lightly spray the paper with more cake-release spray.

2. Use an electric stand mixer to beat all the cake ingredients together until you have a smooth, soft batter. Divide the mixture evenly between the three tins and ensure the surface of the batter is smooth. Bake for 20 minutes until the cakes are golden on top and spring back when lightly pressed with a finger. Leave to cool in the tin for 15 minutes, then turn out onto wire racks to cool completely.

3. Make the Marshmallow Crème as described on page 17, but double the ingredients and mixing times. Divide into 4 separate bowls, cover and set aside. Cream together the softened butter and icing sugar to make a buttercream. Add the buttercream to the Marshmallow Crème a tablespoon at a time until fully combined. Divide the buttercrème in half between 2 bowls. Beat the vanilla bean paste into one half to give the white vanilla filling and topping. Divide the remaining buttercrème in half again to give two quarter portions. Beat 10g (½oz) of the freeze-dried raspberry powder into one of these portions and 5g (⅛oz) into the other – this will give you 2 pink raspberry toppings in slightly different shades.

4. To assemble the cake, put one sponge layer on a serving plate or stand. Spread the cake with a layer of the white vanilla mallow buttercrème and top with fresh raspberries. Spread a thin layer of raspberry jam on top of the next sponge layer and place it jam side down on top of the fresh raspberry layer. Repeat this process until the cake is assembled.

5. Now you are ready to ice the cake. Spoon the darkest pink buttercrème into a piping bag fitted with a wide nozzle and pipe the buttercrème roughly around the sides of the bottom 40 per cent of the cake. Use an angled palette knife and, turning the cake slowly, smooth the buttercrème around the cake. Repeat with the lighter pink raspberry buttercrème and finally with the remaining white vanilla buttercrème until the cake is fully iced. The three tones of buttercrème create an ombre effect going from dark pink at the base to pale pink and then white on the top. Stored in a tall cake tin, this cake will last for up to 3 days.

Frozen Banana and Marshmallow Popsicles

MAKES 6

2 large marshmallows (flavour of
  your choice)
3 large ripe bananas
100g (3½oz) milk chocolate, melted
100g (3½ oz) white chocolate,
  melted

Ice-lolly moulds
Wooden sticks
Piping bags

Banana freezes so easily and makes a fantastic instant, creamy ice cream. We combine ours with marshmallow to create a sweeter pop with a lighter texture. We like to use peanut butter mallows but vanilla would also work, as would fruity flavours.

1. Use a food processor to blend the bananas and marshmallows together until smooth. Pour into your ice-lolly moulds and add the lolly sticks. Put the popsicles in the freezer, standing upright, and leave to freeze for at least 4 hours.

2. Once frozen, remove the moulds from the freezer and run under hot tap water to loosen and release. Lay the popsicles flat on a baking tray lined with greaseproof paper.

3. Fill two piping bags with the melted chocolate and gently drizzle each popsicle with strands of milk and white chocolate. Put the baking tray back in the freezer to firm up the chocolate. You can then return the popsicles to the freezer to serve later or enjoy them straightaway.

Elderflower and Berry Ices

MAKES 6

3 Elderflower and Blackcurrant
  Marshmallows (see page 74)
Fresh redcurrants
300ml (10fl oz) elderflower drink,
  made up using manufacturer's
  instructions

Ice lolly moulds
Wooden sticks

A delicious treat on a hot day – these ices have a great contrasting texture with the frozen mallows and fresh fruit. They can also be more of a grown-up treat if you make the elderflower cordial with sparkling wine instead of water.

1. Slice the marshmallows into long thin strips ensuring both flavour layers are intact.

2. Fill each ice-lolly mould with a mixture of the mallow pieces and redcurrants and top up with the elderflower drink.

3. Add the lolly sticks and freeze for 4 hours until completely set.

4. When ready to serve, run hot tap water over the moulds to loosen and release the ices.

CHAPTER THREE

AFTERNOON TEA

French Almond and Sour Cherry Mallows

**MAKES 36 LARGE
MARSHMALLOWS**

2 large egg whites
150ml (5fl oz) boiling water
30g (1⅛oz) powdered gelatine
500g (1lb 2oz) white granulated
  or caster sugar
4 teaspoons golden syrup
200ml (6fl oz) cold water
1 teaspoon French almond extract
25g (1oz) chopped freeze-dried
  cherries or dried unsweetened
  sour cherries
30g (1⅛ oz) toasted flaked almonds
Cornflour and icing sugar, for
  dusting

23 x 23cm (9 x 9 inch) baking
  tin lightly sprayed with cake-
  release spray

These mallows are called The Kensington as they are made using French almond extract – South Kensington is also know as Little Paris due to the abundance of French schools, cafés and brasseries. This has to be one of our most popular flavours – slightly reminiscent of a cherry bakewell but much more refined. The sour cherry cuts through the sweet almondy mallow and the toasted flaked almonds on top give it a little crunch and texture – c'est si bon!

1. Whisk the egg whites using an electric stand mixer to stiff peaks and set aside. Pour the boiling water into a bowl, evenly sprinkle over the powdered gelatine and gently whisk until fully dissolved.

2. Use the sugar, golden syrup and cold water to make a hard-ball sugar syrup, add the gelatine and combine with the egg whites until they turn glossy as described on page 10. Keep mixing on full speed for 10 minutes until the mixture is the same consistency as lightly whipped double cream. Add the almond extract and whisk for a final 30 seconds until fully combined.

3. Turn off the mixer and pour half the marshmallow into the prepared baking tin. Scatter over the chopped dried cherries and pour over the remaining mallow mixture. Make sure it is evenly spread out, scatter with flaked almonds and cover with cling film. Leave to set as described on page 11.

4. Turn out and cut the mallow as described on page 11.

5. Enjoy these mallows straightaway or keep in an airtight container for 2 weeks.

Rosewater Marshmallows
with Pistachio Praline

MAKES 36 LARGE MARSHMALLOWS

2 large egg whites

120ml (4fl oz) boiling water

30g (1⅛oz) powdered gelatine

500g (1lb 2oz) white granulated or caster sugar

1 tablespoon golden syrup

200ml (7fl oz) cold water

1½ teaspoons rosewater

2 teaspoons natural pink food colouring

1 teaspoon natural blue food colouring

50g (1¾oz) Pistachio Praline, finely chopped (see page 18)

Cornflour and icing sugar, for dusting

Edible rose petals and chopped pistachios, to decorate

23 x 23cm (9 x 9 inch) baking tin lightly sprayed with cake-release spray

This rosewater marshmallow is floral and sweet, which contrasts perfectly with the slightly salted homemade pistachio praline layer. We like to top ours with edible rose petals and chopped pistachios.

1. Whisk the egg whites using an electric stand mixer to stiff peaks and set aside. Pour the boiling water into a bowl, evenly sprinkle over the powdered gelatine and gently whisk until fully dissolved.

2. Use the sugar, golden syrup and cold water to make a hard-ball sugar syrup, add the gelatine and combine with the egg whites until they turn glossy as described on page 10. Keep mixing on full speed for 10 minutes until the mixture is the same consistency as lightly whipped double cream. Add the rosewater and colourings and whisk for a further 30 seconds until fully combined.

3. Turn off the mixer and pour half the mallow mixture into the greased baking tin. Sprinkle with the praline, then top with the rest of the mallow mixture. Make sure it is evenly spread out and cover with cling film. Leave to set as described on page 11.

4. Turn out and cut the mallow as described on page 11.

5. To serve, sprinkle the marshmallows with edible rose petals and chopped pistachios – perfect to go with a sophisticated afternoon tea! Enjoy these mallows straightaway or keep in an airtight container for 2 weeks.

White Chocolate Teacake
with a Rosewater Mallow Filling

These teacakes are so pretty and sophisticated. The pink rose mallow crème in the centre looks fantastic inside the pale green, white chocolate shell, although the green food colouring is optional if you prefer the creamy white colour. We also like to top each teacake with finely chopped pistachios and edible rose petals.

MAKES 6

300g (10½oz) white chocolate, chopped
¼ teaspoon natural green food colouring (optional), plus a few extra dashes

For the biscuit

50g (1¾oz) wholemeal flour
50g (1¾oz) plain flour, plus extra for dusting
Pinch of salt
½ teaspoon baking powder
25g (1oz) caster sugar
25g (1oz) unsalted butter
2 tablespoons semi-skimmed milk

For the rose marshmallow filling

1 quantity of Marshmallow Crème (see page 17)
¼ teaspoon natural pink food colouring
½ teaspoon rosewater

To decorate

1 tablespoon finely chopped pistachios
1 teaspoon edible dried rose petals, to decorate

7.5cm (3 inch) round cutter
Silicone mould for 6 teacakes
Piping bags fitted with plain and small nozzle

1 First make the biscuits. Put the flours, salt, baking powder and caster sugar in a bowl and rub in the butter with your fingertips until it resembles breadcrumbs. Add the milk and stir everything together to form a smooth ball.

2. On a floured work surface roll out the dough to about 4mm (⅛ inch) thick. Cut out 6 rounds with a 7.5cm (3 inch) round cutter, place them on a flat surface and chill in the fridge for 10 minutes. Meanwhile, preheat the oven to 190°C/170°C fan/375°F/Gas Mark 5.

3. Transfer the chilled biscuits to a baking tray and bake for 10–12 minutes. When they're done, remove from the oven and leave to cool on a wire rack.

4. Next melt the chocolate. Put approximately 1 litre (35fl oz) water in a large saucepan and place a large heatproof bowl over the pan. Bring the water up to a steady simmer, then turn off the heat. Place 200g (7oz) of the chopped chocolate into the bowl and leave for 5–10 minutes, stirring occasionally, allowing the residual heat to melt the chocolate. Melting chocolate at a lower temperature results in a glossier finish. Stir in the green colouring, if using.

5 Get your teacake mould and coat the inside of each mould with the melted chocolate – we find it's best using a tablespoon's worth of chocolate in each half-sphere. Use the back of a spoon to work the chocolate up and around the sides of the spheres, adding more chocolate if necessary. The chocolate needs to be thick enough to hold the shape of the teacake but not so thick that you end up with a chocolate-heavy teacake.

6. You should have some melted chocolate leftover. Take the cooled biscuits and dip one side in the remaining melted chocolate and set aside on a tray to harden.

7. Now, make the marshmallow filling – follow the Marshmallow Crème recipe as described on page 17. Once the crème is made, add the pink colouring and rosewater, mixing them in for 30 seconds.

8. Spoon the mallow filling into a piping bag with a plain wide nozzle and pipe the mallow into each of the 6 chocolate-coated moulds, remembering to leave a 4mm (⅛ inch) gap at the top so the biscuit will sit flush. Carefully place the cooled biscuits on top of the mallow, chocolate side down. The chocolate will stop the biscuit going soft.

9. Melt the remaining 100g (3½oz) chocolate and add a little green colouring if using. Transfer to a piping bag with a small nozzle. Carefully pipe around the circumference of the biscuit and pipe a small amount on top of each biscuit. Spread the chocolate evenly over the biscuit using a palette knife. Leave the teacakes to cool and set overnight or for at least 8 hours; do not refrigerate, as the chocolate will lose its glossy shine.

10. Carefully remove the teacakes from the moulds, trying not to handle them too much as fingerprints will mark the glossy dome. Decorate with the chopped pistachios and edible rose petals. These teacakes will last for 2 days.

Cherry and Almond 'Fifteen' Biscuits

MAKES 30 BISCUITS

125g (4½oz) French Almond and Sour Cherry Mallows (*see page 50*) – about 5 pieces

15 digestive biscuits, crushed

15 glacé cherries, halved

225ml (7¾fl oz) sweetened condensed milk

150g (5½oz) organic desiccated coconut

These refrigerator biscuits originate from Northern Ireland. The cherries in the mallows add extra sourness and the almond oil and toasted almond add flavour and crunch. This would work as well with the Vanilla (see page 14) or Raspberry and Coconut Marshmallows (see page 27).

1. Use scissors to cut the marshmallows into eighths – you may need to dust the freshly cut mallow with a little bit of cornflour and icing sugar to make it easier to handle. Arrange on a tray or plate, slightly set apart so the pieces are not touching, and place in the freezer for 20 minutes.

2. Combine the crushed biscuits and cherry halves in a large mixing bowl. Gradually stir in the condensed milk, then add the chilled marshmallow pieces and stir until fully combined – you may need to use your hands for this bit!

3. Spread a generous layer of the desiccated coconut on a clean work surface. Split the fifteens mixture in half and place one half on top of the coconut. Use your hands to form the mixture into a neat sausage shape about 5cm (2 inches) in diameter, making sure it is well coated with coconut. Wrap in cling film and chill in the fridge for 2–3 hours. Repeat with the other half of the mixture.

4. Once chilled, unwrap the two sausages and slice into 15 pieces each – be careful not to slice too thinly as the biscuits may crumble and break. The biscuits will keep for 1 week stored in an airtight container in the fridge.

Assam Tea with Rosewater Marshmallow Float

This is inspired by Russian tea drinking, where it is popular to add a spoonful of jam to sweeten your tea – rose petal and strawberry being favourites. The Assam tea has a strong brisk flavour – make without milk and serve with a rosewater marshmallow for a hot sweet and floral treat.

MAKES 6 CUPS

6 Assam tea bags or 6 teaspoons loose
   leaf Assam tea
800ml (27fl oz) freshly boiled water
6 Rosewater Marshmallows *(see page 52)*,
   made as per the recipe but omitting
   the decoration

1. Prepare the tea according to the packet instructions (we use 1 teaspoon of loose leaf tea per person). Use a teapot and make sure to warm the pot first. Use freshly boiled water and leave the tea to brew for 4 minutes before pouring into fine bone china tea cups.

2. Serve with a large rosewater marshmallow. Guests should gently place the marshmallow onto the surface of the tea and allow the sugary marshmallow to slowly melt into the strong Assam brew.

Lavender and Raspberry Marshmallows

MAKES 36 LARGE MARSHMALLOWS

For the lavender layer

1 large egg white

75ml (2¾fl oz) boiling water

15g (½oz) powdered gelatine

250g (9oz) white granulated or caster sugar

2 teaspoons golden syrup

100ml (3½fl oz) cold water

¼ teaspoon lavender extract

2 teaspoons natural blue food colouring

1½ teaspoons natural pink food colouring

For the raspberry layer

1 large egg white

150ml (5fl oz) cold water

20g (¾oz) freeze-dried raspberry powder

65ml (2½fl oz) boiling water

17g (¾oz) powdered gelatine

265g (9½oz) white granulated or caster sugar

2 teaspoons golden syrup

To finish

1 teaspoon freeze-dried raspberry powder

15g edible lavender buds

Cornflour and icing sugar, for dusting

23 x 23cm (9 x 9 inch) baking tin lightly sprayed with cake-release spray

Lavender on its own can be rather floral. We once had a fantastic dessert in Provence, which was a frozen parfait that combined local lavender and raspberry – the result was so delicious that we have recreated it here for a marshmallow. It also has the added bonus of being exceptionally colourful and pretty.

1. To make the lavender layer, whisk the egg white using an electric stand mixer to stiff peaks and set aside. Pour the boiling water into a bowl, evenly sprinkle over the powdered gelatine and gently whisk until fully dissolved.

2. Use the sugar, golden syrup and water to make a hard-ball sugar syrup, add the gelatine and combine with the egg white until it turns glossy as described on page 10. Keep mixing on full speed for 5 minutes, stop the mixer and add the lavender extract and food colourings. Turn the mixer back on to full speed for another 30 seconds until the mixture is a pretty pale purple colour and the same consistency as lightly whipped double cream.

3. Turn off the mixer and pour the marshmallow into the baking tin. Make sure it is evenly spread out, cover with cling film and set aside while you make the next layer.

4. To make the raspberry layer, whisk the egg white to stiff peaks using an electric stand mixer and set aside. Add 50ml (1¾fl oz) of the cold water to the raspberry powder, thoroughly stir and set aside. Pour the boiling water into a bowl, evenly sprinkle over the powdered gelatine and gently stir in with a whisk until fully dissolved.

5. Use the sugar, golden syrup and remaining cold water to make a hard-ball sugar syrup, add the gelatine and combine with the egg white until it turns glossy as described on page 10. Keep mixing on full speed for 3 minutes, stop the mixer and add the raspberry/water mixture. Turn the mixer back on to full speed for a further 2 minutes until the mixture is the same consistency as lightly whipped double cream.

6. Pour on top of the lavender layer, making sure the surface is even, then sprinkle the surface with a teaspoon of freeze-fried raspberry powder and the lavender buds. Cover with cling film and leave to set as described on page 11.

7. Turn out and cut the mallow as described on page 11.

8. Enjoy these mallows straightaway or keep in an airtight container for 2 weeks.

Walnut Meringue 'French Kisses'
with Coffee Marshmallow Buttercrème Filling

We call these French kisses because they are so much more than a normal meringue kiss! Two crispy chewy meringue kisses scattered with walnuts and sandwiched with coffee marshmallow buttercrème – totally cute and moreish!

MAKES 25

For the meringue
3 large egg whites
50g (1¾oz) golden caster sugar
100g (3½oz) caster sugar
Handful of chopped walnuts
100g (3½oz) dark chocolate, melted

For the coffee marshmallow buttercrème
1 quantity of Marshmallow Crème
  (see page 17)
100g (3½oz) icing sugar
150g (5½oz) unsalted butter
2 teaspoons strong instant coffee
  dissolved in 1 teaspoon hot water

Piping bags fitted with a star nozzle
  and wide plain nozzle

1. Preheat the oven to 200°C/180°C fan/400°F/Gas Mark 6.

2. Make the meringue first. Whisk the egg whites using an electric stand mixer until they form stiff peaks. Continue whisking and add the sugar, a tablespoon at a time, until fully incorporated. Continue whisking for a further 8 minutes until the meringue mixture is stiff, glossy and not grainy.

3. Turn the oven down to 110°C/90°C fan/200°F/Gas Mark ¼. Using small dabs of the meringue mix in each corner, stick greaseproof paper down onto 2 large flat baking trays. Transfer the meringue mix to a piping bag fitted with a star nozzle. Pipe the meringue into kisses, about 4cm (1½ inches) in diameter. Scatter the meringues gently with the chopped walnuts.

4. Bake the meringues in the oven for 35 minutes, then turn off the oven and leave the meringues in the oven to cool completely. Once cool, take each meringue and carefully dip the flat edge into the melted dark chocolate. Leave the chocolate to completely set.

5. To make the coffee filling, make the Marshmallow Crème as described on page 17 and set aside. Cream together the icing sugar and butter using an electric stand mixer. Once smooth and fluffy, add the coffee and mix until completely combined. Beat in the Marshmallow Crème.

6. To assemble, take 2 meringue kisses and sandwich them together with a generous blob of the marshmallow buttercrème – you can use a teaspoon or a piping bag if you want to be extra neat. For added crunch you can now roll the buttercrème edges of the French kisses in extra chopped walnuts.

Flavour Variations: Try pistachio kisses and rose crème; lime kisses with lemon crème; or coconut kisses with raspberry crème.

Earl Grey Tea and Lemon Marshmallow Sandwich Biscuits

MAKES 40 SMALL BISCUITS

260g (9¼oz) plain flour

1 tablespoon Earl Grey tea leaves (loose or from bags)

Pinch of salt

225g (8½oz) unsalted butter, softened

65g (2oz) icing sugar

1 tablespoon unwaxed grated lemon zest

200g (7oz) white chocolate, melted

75g (2¾oz) lemon curd (freshly made, *see page 33* or shop-bought)

1 quantity of Marshmallow Fluff (*see page 17*)

These delicious little butter biscuits flavoured with fragrant Earl Grey tea and lemon can be eaten as they are, but we like to sandwich them with white chocolate, zingy lemon curd and soft marshmallow fluff.

1. Mix together the flour, tea and salt and set aside.

2. Using an electric stand mixer set to medium, cream together the butter, sugar and lemon zest until pale and fluffy. After 3 minutes, reduce the speed to low and add the flour and tea mixture. Mix until combined.

3. Divide the dough into two and transfer each piece on to sheets of greaseproof paper (about 30 x 30cm/12 x 12 inches). Use the paper to carefully shape the dough into two even logs, about 4cm (1½ inches) in diameter. Wrap the paper neatly around each log, then wrap again with cling film. Pop each log into the freezer for about 1 hour.

4. Preheat the oven to 200°C/180°C fan/400°F/Gas Mark 6. Remove the logs from the freezer and unwrap them. Cut the logs into thin 4mm (⅛ inch) slices and space 4cm (1½ inches) apart on a baking sheet lined with greaseproof paper. Bake in the oven for 10–12 minutes or until the edges just turn golden. Leave to cool on wire racks.

5. Once cool, dip the flat edge of each biscuit in the melted white chocolate, then pop them in the fridge to set hard.

6. Once the chocolate is set, you can assemble your biscuits. Take half the biscuits and spoon a small amount of lemon curd into the middle of the chocolate sides.

7. Make the Marshmallow Fluff as described on page 17 and pipe a small blob on top of the lemon curd. Take another biscuit and sandwich together, with both chocolate sides facing together. Enjoy with a fresh cup of hot Earl Grey tea.

Mini Lavender and Rose Whoopee Pies

MAKES 30 MINI PIES

For the cookies

275g (9¾oz) plain flour
¾ teaspoon bicarbonate of soda
½ teaspoon salt
1 medium egg
150g (5½oz) caster sugar
75g (2¾oz) unsalted butter, melted
150ml (5fl oz) buttermilk
½ teaspoon lavender extract
2 teaspoons natural pink food
    colouring
3 teaspoons natural blue food
    colouring
Edible lavender buds (optional)

For the rosewater marshmallow buttercrème

1 quantity of Marshmallow Crème
    (see page 17)
100g (3½oz) icing sugar
150g (5½oz) unsalted butter,
    softened
¼ teaspoon rosewater
½ teaspoon natural pink food
    colouring
¼ teaspoon natural blue food
    colouring
Rose petal jam

Piping bag fitted with a wide nozzle

The ultimate floral treat for an afternoon tea – super delicate and pretty, these dainty whoopee pies are flavoured with both rosewater and lavender extract.

1. Preheat the oven to 200°C/180°C fan/400°F/Gas Mark 6 and line 2 large baking trays with greaseproof paper. Sift together the flour, bicarbonate of soda and salt into a medium bowl and set aside.

2. Whisk the egg and sugar for 3–4 minutes with an electric stand mixer until light and fluffy. Add the melted butter, buttermilk, lavender extract and colourings and whisk until combined. Fold in the flour mixture.

3. Spoon a teaspoonful of the dough for each cookie onto the baking trays. They need to be spaced about 2.5cm (1 inch) apart so you should fit about 30 onto each baking tray. Sprinkle the tops of the cookies with edible lavender buds, if using.

4. Bake for 6–7 minutes or until the cookies spring back when lightly touched. Transfer from the baking sheets to wire racks and leave to cool.

5. To make the rosewater marshmallow buttercrème, make the Marshmallow Crème as described on page 17 and set aside. Cream together the icing sugar and butter using an electric stand mixer. Once smooth and fluffy, add the rosewater and food colourings and mix until completely combined. Beat in the Marshmallow Crème.

6. Brush the flat side of each cookie with a little rose petal jam and allow it to sink into the cookie. Spoon the mallow filling into a piping bag fitted with a wide nozzle and use it to pipe the filling onto the flat sides of half the cookies. Sandwich with another cookie to make 30 whoopee pies.

Lemon and Fiery Ginger Roulade
with Crème Fraîche Marshmallow Filling

The key to this roulade is using crème fraîche in the marshmallow filling to create sourness and take away from the sugary sweet marshmallow crème. Combined with the sharp lemon drizzle and plenty of fiery crystallized ginger (we always buy the extra hot version), it's a fantastic combination.

SERVES 10–12

For the roulade sponge
130g (4½oz) plain flour
1½ teaspoons ground ginger
¾ teaspoon baking powder
Grated zest of 1 lemon
¼ teaspoon salt
165g (5¾oz) soft light brown sugar
6 medium eggs, separated
45g (1½oz) butter, melted
Icing sugar, for dusting

For the filling
⅔ quantity of Marshmallow Crème
 (see page 17)
100g (3½oz) unsalted butter
65g (2oz) icing sugar
Juice and grated zest of ½ lemon
200g (7oz) crème fraîche
30g (1⅛oz) chopped fiery
 crystallized ginger

For the drizzle topping
Juice and grated zest of ½ lemon
100g (3½oz) icing sugar
15g (½oz) sliced crystallized ginger
1 tablespoon golden demerara
 sugar

1. First, make the roulade sponge. Preheat the oven to 200°C/180°C fan/350°F/Gas Mark 4. Grease a 35 x 30cm (14 x 12 inch) baking tray and line it with greaseproof paper, then grease and flour the paper. Set the tray aside.

2. Stir together the flour, ground ginger, baking powder, lemon zest and salt in a mixing bowl and set aside. Beat the sugar and egg yolks together in a separate bowl for about 3 minutes until thick and light in colour. Add the melted butter and beat for a further 30 seconds until fully combined, then fold in the flour mixture.

3. Whisk the egg whites in the clean bowl of an electric stand mixer until they form stiff peaks. Fold one-third of the beaten egg whites into the egg yolk and flour mixture to lighten the mixture. Fold in the remaining egg whites. Pour the batter into the prepared tray and spread evenly. Bake for 12 minutes or until the top of the sponge springs back when lightly touched.

4. Meanwhile, place a clean tea towel on a kitchen surface and dust with icing sugar. Once the sponge is cooked, remove from the oven and turn out straight onto the towel. Remove the greaseproof paper. While still warm, gently roll the towel and the sponge up together into a spiral starting at one long edge. Leave to cool, seam side down, on a wire rack.

5. Meanwhile, make the filling. Make the Marshmallow Crème as described on page 17, but reduce the ingredients and mixing times by one-third. Cover and set aside. Cream together the butter and the icing sugar until smooth and fluffy to form a buttercream. Add the buttercream to the Marshmallow Crème a tablespoon at a time, beating in fully after each addition of buttercream.

6. Unroll the cooled sponge from the tea towel. Brush the inside of the sponge with the lemon juice. Spread the crème fraîche evenly over the inside of the sponge, then spread half the mallow filling on top. Sprinkle over the chopped crystallized ginger and lemon zest. Carefully roll the roulade back up. Slice off the ends to create a neat finish and place seam-side down on your serving plate.

7. To make the drizzle topping, mix the lemon juice and icing sugar together until smooth and runny. Carefully pour the drizzle over the top of the roulade allowing it to run down the sides. To decorate, scatter with sliced crystallized ginger, lemon zest and a sprinkle of golden demerara sugar for extra crunch. To serve, cut into slices and serve with any remaining mallow buttercrème. This roulade will keep for 3 days.

Chai Tea Marshmallows

MAKES 36 LARGE MARSHMALLOWS

2 large egg whites
450ml (16fl oz) boiling hot black chai tea (made with 6 chai tea bags)
30g (1⅛oz) powdered gelatine
2 cardamon pods
¾ teaspoon ground ginger
½ teaspoon ground cinnamon
⅛ teaspoon ground cloves
500g (1lb 2oz) white granulated or caster sugar
4 teaspoons golden syrup

For the topping

200g (7oz) good-quality milk or dark chocolate, melted
50g (1¾oz) chopped raw pistachio kernels

23 x 23cm (9 x 9 inch) baking tin sprayed with cake-release spray

These marshmallows, with their distinctive spices, are inspired by the sweet spicy tea we drank throughout our travels around India. Back in London, we still regularly drink chai tea and these mallows topped with chocolate and chopped pistachios are a great addition to an afternoon tea spread.

1. Whisk the egg whites using an electric stand mixer to stiff peaks and set aside. Pour 150ml (5fl oz) of the boiling hot chai tea into a bowl, evenly sprinkle over the powdered gelatine and gently whisk until fully dissolved. Crack open the cardamom pods in a pestle and mortar, discard the outer skins and grind the interior black seeds. Mix with the other ground spices and add to the gelatine and tea mix.

2. Use the sugar, golden syrup and remaining tea to make a hard-ball sugar syrup, add the gelatine and combine with the egg whites until they turn glossy as described on page 10. Keep mixing on full speed for 10 minutes until the mixture is the same consistency as lightly whipped double cream.

3. Turn off the mixer and pour the marshmallow into the baking tin. Make sure it is evenly spread out and cover with cling film. Leave to set as described on page 11.

4. Turn out and cut the mallow as described on page 11. Melt the chocolate as described on page 22 (step 6). Dip the top surface of each mallow into the chocolate and sprinkle with the chopped pistachios. Leave the chocolate to set.

5. Enjoy these mallows straightaway or keep in an airtight container for 2 weeks.

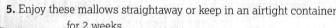

Flavour variation

Earl Grey Tea and Lemon Marshmallows

Turn this into a fantastic Earl Grey tea-flavoured marshmallow by making the recipe as above with the following changes: replace the chai tea with the same amount of Earl Grey tea, increase the gelatine to 34g (1¼oz), omit the spices and decoration, add the juice of 2 lemons to the gelatine mix once it has cooled and scatter the surface with grated lemon zest.

Raspberry Ripple and Vanilla Mallow Jellies

SERVES 6

½ quantity of Madagascan Vanilla Marshmallows (*see page 14*)
½ teaspoon natural pink food colouring
½ teaspoon natural red food colouring
200g (7oz) fresh raspberries
Cornflour and icing sugar, for dusting

6 small jelly moulds, lightly sprayed with cake-release spray

These fun little marshmallow jellies are reminiscent of raspberry ripple ice cream. Serve with a cake fork and as you cut into them the fresh raspberry centre will be revealed.

1. Make the Madagascan Vanilla Marshmallows following the instructions on page 14, up to the end of step 2, halving the ingredients and mixing times. Once the mixture is ready, lightly fold in the red and pink food colouring to create a raspberry ripple affect.

2. Gently spoon the mixture into each mould until half full each. Gently place the raspberries on top of the marshmallow mixture, pressing them in slightly, and top up with the remaining marshmallow mixture.

3. Cover each mould with cling film and set aside overnight or for 8 hours at room temperature to allow the marshmallow to firm up. If you are short on time, pop it in the fridge for 2 hours.

4. Lightly dust the base of each marshmallow with a 50:50 mix of cornflour and icing sugar. Gently turn out the jelly moulds onto individual plates and serve. These marshmallow jellies need to be eaten within 1–2 days due to the fresh raspberry.

Strawberry and Black Pepper Mallows

MAKES 36 LARGE MARSHMALLOWS

2 medium egg whites
90ml (3fl oz) boiling water
36g (1¼oz) powdered gelatine
½ teaspoon freshly ground black pepper, plus extra for sprinkling
500g (1lb 2oz) white granulated or caster sugar
4 teaspoons golden syrup
250ml (8½fl oz) strawberry purée
½ teaspoon natural pink food colouring
Cornflour and icing sugar, for dusting

23 x 23cm (9 x 9 inch) square baking tin lightly sprayed with cake-release spray

This is an unexpected take on a strawberry marshmallow – the black pepper gives a good kick and really complements the flavour.

1. Whisk the egg whites using an electric stand mixer to stiff peaks and set aside. Pour the boiling water into a bowl, evenly sprinkle over the powdered gelatine and ½ teaspoon freshly ground black pepper and gently whisk until fully dissolved.

2. Use the sugar, golden syrup and 150ml (5fl oz) of the strawberry purée to make a hard-ball sugar syrup, add the gelatine and combine with the egg whites until they turn glossy as described on page 10. Keep mixing on full speed for 5 minutes, stop the mixer and add the remaining purée. Turn the mixer back on to full speed for a further 5 minutes until the mixture is the same consistency as lightly whipped double cream. Add the food colouring and mix for a final 30 seconds until fully combined.

3. Turn off the mixer and pour the marshmallow into the prepared baking tin. Make sure it is evenly spread out, then sprinkle a light coating of black pepper on top. Cover with cling film and leave to set as described on page 11.

4. Turn out and cut the mallow as described on page 11. Enjoy these mallows straightaway or keep in an airtight container for 2 weeks.

Strawberry and White Choc Mallow Crispy Cakes

MAKES 24 SQUARES

45g (1½oz) unsalted butter
300g (10½oz) large strawberry marshmallows (*see page 22*) – about 14
180g (6oz) puffed rice cereal
100g (3½oz) white chocolate, melted
50g (1¾oz) freeze-dried sliced strawberries

Using strawberry marshmallow and white chocolate this is an update on the traditional childhood milk chocolate rice crispy cakes.

1. Melt the butter in a large saucepan, add the marshmallows and stir until melted. Stir in the puffed rice cereal. Pour the mixture into a baking tin lightly sprayed with cake-release spray and press down into an even layer. Pop into the fridge to set.

2. Once set, turn out of the tin and cut into 24 even squares. Spoon the melted chocolate into a piping bag and drizzle the squares with white chocolate. Scatter with freeze-dried sliced strawberries to finish. Once the chocolate is set, stack on a plate and serve. These will keep for 2 days in an airtight container.

Layered Elderflower and Blackcurrant Marshmallows

**MAKES 36 LARGE
MARSHMALLOWS**

For the elderflower layer

1 medium egg white
50ml (2fl oz) elderflower cordial
60ml (2¼fl oz) boiling water
18g (¾oz) powdered gelatine
250g (9oz) white granulated or
   caster sugar
2 teaspoons golden syrup
100ml (3½fl oz) cold water
1 teaspoon natural green food
   colouring

For the blackcurrant layer

1 medium egg white
140ml (5fl oz) cold water
15g (½oz) freeze-dried blackcurrant
   powder
65ml (2½fl oz) boiling water
18g (¾oz) powdered gelatine
250g (9oz) white granulated or
   caster sugar
2 teaspoons golden syrup
100ml (3½fl oz) water

To finish

5g (⅛oz) freeze-dried blackcurrant
   powder
Cornflour and icing sugar,
   for dusting

23 x 23cm (9 x 9 inch) baking
   tin lightly sprayed with cake-
   release spray

Our original double layer marshmallow – floral green elderflower topped with vibrant fruity purple blackcurrant.

1. To make the elderflower layer, whisk the egg white and elderflower cordial together using an electric stand mixer to stiff peaks and set aside. Pour the boiling water into a bowl, evenly sprinkle over the powdered gelatine and gently whisk until dissolved.

2. Use the sugar, golden syrup and cold water to make a hard-ball sugar syrup, add the gelatine and combine with the egg white until it turns glossy as described on page 10. Keep mixing on full speed for 3 minutes, stop the mixer and add the colouring. Turn the mixer back on to full speed for another 2 minutes until the mixture is a pretty pale green colour and the same consistency as lightly whipped double cream.

3. Turn off the mixer and pour the marshmallow into the baking tin. Make sure it is evenly spread out, cover with cling film and set aside while you make the next layer.

4. To make the blackcurrant layer, whisk the egg white to stiff peaks using an electric stand mixer and set aside. Add 40ml (1½fl oz) of the cold water to the blackcurrant powder, thoroughly stir and set aside. Pour the boiling water into a bowl, evenly sprinkle over the powdered gelatine and gently stir in with a whisk until fully dissolved.

5. Use the sugar, golden syrup and remaining cold water to make a hard-ball sugar syrup, add the gelatine and combine with the egg white until it turns glossy as described on page 10. Keep mixing on full speed for 3 minutes, stop the mixer and add the blackcurrant/water mixture. Turn the mixer back on to full speed for a further 2 minutes until the mixture is the same consistency as lightly whipped double cream.

6. Pour on top of the elderflower layer, making sure the surface is even and finish by sprinkling the surface with the blackcurrant powder. Cover with cling film and leave to set as described on page 11.

7. Turn out and cut the mallow as described on page 11.

8. Enjoy these mallows straightaway or keep in an airtight container for 2 weeks.

Marshmallow Kir Royale

A Kir Royale is our aperitif of choice on our yearly summer holiday to the south of France. Traditionally made with crème de cassis we top ours off with a blackcurrant and elderflower mallow for a fun alternative.

MAKES 6 GLASSES

1 bottle of chilled champagne
50ml (2fl oz) Crème de Cassis
6 Elderflower and Blackcurrant Marshmallows (*see opposite*)

1. Divide the cassis between 6 champagne saucers. Top up with the chilled champagne. Top each glass with an elderflower and blackcurrant marshmallow to finish and … voila!

CHAPTER FOUR

S'MORES AND MALLOW POPS

Indoor S'mores

S'mores are a traditional campfire snack in the States and are usually made with shop-bought mallows, a piece of chocolate and graham crackers (the US version of digestive biscuits). They are best described as a very messy, very sticky, molten marshmallow sandwich. They are truly irresistible!

MAKES 8 S'MORES

16 thin biscuits (shop-bought
   or see recipe below)
8 thin rectangular pieces of
   chocolate
4 large marshmallows (flavour of
   your choice), cut in half

Kitchen blowtorch

MAKES 32 CRACKERS

190g (6½oz) plain white flour, plus
   extra for dusting
130g (4½oz) plain wholemeal flour
65g (2¼oz) wheatgerm
½ teaspoon salt
1 teaspoon bicarbonate of soda
1 teaspoon ground cinnamon
200g (7oz) unsalted butter
165g (5¾oz) soft light brown sugar
2 tablespoons runny honey

5 sheets of greaseproof paper
   measuring 30 x 25cm
   (12 x 10 inches)
Fluted pastry wheel

Making indoor s'mores

1. Arrange 8 of your thin biscuits on a baking tray and place a piece of chocolate on top of each one. Lightly blowtorch the surface of the chocolate to start it melting.

2. Add a halved marshmallow and lightly blowtorch its top and sides, allowing the surface to soufflé up a little.

3. Sandwich with the remaining biscuits and enjoy immediately – watch out, it will be very hot for a while so take care!

Homemade Graham crackers

1. Use a pencil to draw a 24 x 20cm (9½ x 8 inch) rectangle on 4 of the greaseproof paper sheets, making sure the lines extend to the edges of the paper to from a grid. Preheat the oven to 200°C/180°C fan/350°F/Gas Mark 6. Whisk the flours, wheatgerm, salt, bicarbonate of soda and cinnamon together in a bowl and set aside.

2. Put the butter, sugar and honey into an electric stand mixer (with the paddle attachment) and mix on a medium speed for 2–3 minutes until pale and fluffy. Then reduce the speed to low and tip in the flour mixture and mix until well combined. Turn the biscuit dough out onto a floured surface and divide into quarters.

3. Place one of the marked sheets of paper, marked side up on the work surface and lightly dust with flour. Place one dough quarter on top of the paper and dust lightly. Place the unmarked sheet of paper on top and roll the dough out between the two sheets of paper to about 3–4mm (⅛ inch) thick. Remove the top sheet and save for the next quarter.

4. Use a fluted pastry wheel to cut along the marked lines, trimming away any excess, to leave you with a rectangular tablet of dough measuring 24 x 20cm (9½ x 8 inches). Use the pastry wheel to cut the long side into 4 and the short side into 2, so you are left with 8 crackers on one tablet of dough. Score each cracker lengthways and widthways by lightly rolling the pastry wheel over the dough. Prick the dough with a fork.

5. Transfer the tablet of dough to a baking tray, keeping it on the greaseproof paper, and bake for 8–9 minutes. Remove from the oven – at this point it's a good idea to run the pastry wheel back over the cuts to help separate the crackers. Leave to cool for 5 minutes before transferring to a wire rack to cool completely. Repeat with the remaining quarters. One cracker, when broken in half, will make one s'more. The crackers can be stored in an airtight container for 3 days.

Tip: Customize the size of your Graham crackers to whatever size you'd like and cut your marshmallows accordingly – mini s'mores are even cuter.

Lemon and Blueberry Milk Chocolate S'mores

Sharp fruity flavours work surprisingly well – combine Layered Lemon and Blueberry Marshmallows (see page 31) with a simple slice of milk chocolate. For an extra lemon hit, use lemon puff biscuits.

Cherry Marshmallow Dark Chocolate S'more Bites

S'mores can be messy – which makes them so appealing to children – but these dainty s'more bites can be served as canapés. Use small dark chocolate biscuits and top with chopped maraschino cherries to make them pop!

Banana and Peanut Butter S'mores

Sprinkle extra peanuts on the blow-torched milk chocolate before adding a slice of
fresh banana and topping with a Peanut Butter Marshmallow (see page 90).

Ultimate Chocolate S'mores

Use white chocolate and cocoa continental biscuits with our Triple Layer White, Milk and Dark Chocolate Marshmallows (see page 98) for the ultimate s'mores satisfaction.

Mallow Pops

MAKES 36 POPS

36 marshmallows (flavour of your
    choice)
400g (14oz) chocolate, melted

Piping bag fitted with a small nozzle
    (optional)
36 plastic or wooden cake pop
    sticks – use wooden if you are
    going to 'toast' the mallows

Mallow pops are a great way to serve marshmallows at events or are perfect to give as gifts or favours. Think about seasonal flavour combinations or choose colours that go with the event or party. The basic principles are the same, but try some of our tried and tested flavour combinations below.

1. Place your marshmallows on a baking tray. If they are already decorated, arrange them decoration side down or with the decoration facing to one side.

2. Use a teaspoon or piping bag fitted with a small nozzle to add a small blob of melted chocolate to the upside of the mallow. Gently insert the pop sticks into the mallow pushing through the melted chocolate. Put the tray of mallows to one side. As the chocolate sets it will secure the stick into the mallow.

3. Once set, keep the pops in an airtight container and serve in bunches at an event, or neatly lined up on a tray. If using for goodie bags or favours insert each pop into a clear cellophane bag and secure with a ribbon.

Flavour variation # Pistachio and Dark Chocolate Mallow Pops

Make a quantity of Pistachio and Milk Chocolate mallows by following the Peanut Butter and Milk Chocolate Mallow recipe on page 90, but use pistachio butter instead of peanut butter. You can make your own pistachio butter by lightly roasting 100g (3½oz) pistachio kernels in a dry frying pan and then blending them with 2 tablespoons vegetable oil and a pinch of salt until smooth. Secure the cake pop stick with melted milk chocolate as above.

Layered Lime and Coconut Mallow Pops

Make a tin of layered lime and coconut mallows by making a half quantity of the Coconut Marshmallows as instructed on page 27 but halving the ingredients, heating and mixing times. Pour into the prepared tin and cover with cling film while you make a lime layer. Make a half batch of Lemon Marshmallows as described on page 30 but replace the lemons with limes, the lemon extract with lime extract and use natural green food colouring instead, halving the ingredients, heating and mixing times. For the pop we dipped the green edge of the mallow in white chocolate and topped with toasted coconut.

Swirled Peach and Prosecco Mallow Pops

Make a batch of Peach and Prosecco Marshmallow mixture (see page 43), but before pouring into the tin gently fold in 1 teaspoon yellow and 1 teaspoon pink nautral food colouring to create a peach skin effect. Once set and cut, top the mallows with dark chocolate and sprinkle with a mixture of chocolate-coated popping candy and bronze sugar decorations. The popping candy will give your guests a surprise!

Violet and Dark Choc Mallow Pops

Make a tin of violet mallows by following the Rosewater Marshmallows on page 52 but omit the pistachio and praline layer and use violet extract instead or rosewater. Top each mallow with a neat disc of dark chocolate and a single crystallized violet petal. Insert the stick into the side of the mallow and once set, pop the mallow into a cellophane bag and secure with a purple ribbon.

CHAPTER FIVE

CROWD PLEASERS

Peanut Butter and Milk Chocolate Mallows

MAKES 36 LARGE MARSHMALLOWS

2 large egg whites
150ml (5fl oz) boiling water
30g (1⅛oz) powdered gelatine
500g (1lb 2oz) white granulated or caster sugar
4 teaspoons golden syrup
200ml (7fl oz) cold water
130g (4½oz) good-quality smooth peanut butter
Cornflour and icing sugar, for dusting

For the topping

200g (7oz) good-quality milk chocolate, chopped
Large handful of chopped salted peanuts

23 x 23cm (9 x 9 inch) baking tin lightly sprayed with cake-release spray

We created this flavour for one of our first ever wedding orders. The couple lived on the other side of Stoke Newington (Stokey) to us and desperately wanted peanut butter mallows for their wedding. It is easily our most popular flavour and always sold out first at Broadway Market. These are absolutely irresistible to anyone who loves peanut butter and that sweet, salty taste makes them truly addictive.

1. Whisk the egg whites using an electric stand mixer to stiff peaks and set aside. Pour the boiling water into a bowl, evenly sprinkle over the powdered gelatine and gently whisk until fully dissolved.

2. Use the sugar, golden syrup and cold water to make a hard-ball sugar syrup, add the gelatine and combine with the egg whites until they turn glossy as described on page 10. Keep mixing while you warm the peanut butter.

3. Put the peanut butter in a small heavy-based saucepan set over a very low heat for 3 minutes until it is loosened and melted, then set aside.

4. After 10 minutes mixing, the mallow mixture should be the same consistency as lightly whipped double cream. Turn off the mixer, pour the warmed peanut butter into the bowl and quickly fold in – do not over fold though as you will loose volume; 3–4 folds of the mix should be sufficient.

5. Pour the marshmallow into the baking tin. Make sure it is evenly spread out and cover with cling film. Leave to set as described on page 11.

6. Turn out and cut the mallow as described on page 11.

7. To make the topping, melt the chocolate as described on page 22 (step 6). Dip the top surface of each mallow in the melted chocolate and then scatter with the chopped peanuts. These chocolate-topped mallows can be served immediately while the chocolate is still warm and sticky or left for a few hours to set.

8. Enjoy these mallows straightaway or keep in an airtight container for 2 weeks.

Sweet and Salty Boozy Banana Split

This easy update on the traditional banana split uses lightly fried bananas to give them a warm sticky glaze. We like to serve ours with good-quality vanilla ice cream, peanut butter marshmallows plus a generous drizzle of warm chocolate and butterscotch sauces, topped with extra chopped peanuts.

SERVES 4

4 large bananas, peeled
2 tablespoons runny honey
30g (1⅛oz) butter
8 Peanut Butter and Milk Chocolate Mallows *(see page 90)*, cut into smaller chunks
4 large scoops of good-quality vanilla ice cream
Large handful of chopped salted peanuts

For the chocolate ganache sauce

50g (1¾oz) white caster sugar
25g (1oz) cocoa powder
85ml (3fl oz) double cream
1 tablespoon golden syrup
45g (1½oz) dark (minimum 50% cocoa solids) chocolate, chopped
15g (½oz) unsalted butter
½ teaspoon vanilla bean paste
Tiny pinch of salt

For the boozy butterscotch sauce

75g (2¾oz) white caster sugar
25ml (1fl oz) hot water
125ml (4fl oz) double cream
1 tablespoon rum or banana liqueur
15g (½oz) cold unsalted butter

1. First, make the chocolate ganache sauce. This recipe makes a medium jug of chocolate ganache sauce – it can be covered and stored in the fridge for 1 week and reheated for another dessert. Combine the sugar and cocoa powder in a heatproof bowl set over a pan of simmering water. Whisk to combine. Add the cream and golden syrup and whisk over the heat for 3–5 minutes until smooth and thick.

2. Add the chocolate, butter, vanilla and salt and stir to combine. Keep warming the sauce for about 2–3 minutes, stirring occasionally, until the chocolate and butter fully melt in and the sauce is super-smooth. Keep this chocolatey sauce warm until you're ready to serve.

3. Next, make the butterscotch sauce. Combine the sugar and hot water in a heavy-based saucepan and cook over a high heat until the sugar has dissolved. Continue to cook, swirling the pan occasionally but never stirring it, until the mixture thickens and turns a wonderful deep amber colour – this should take 5–8 minutes.

4. Remove the pan from the heat and immediately and gently pour in the double cream. Return the pan to a medium heat and cook for a further 5 minutes until the sauce is thick and creamy, stirring occasionally. Remove the pan from the heat and stir in the alcohol and butter. Keep the sauce warm until you're ready to serve.

5. Now it is time to assemble your banana split. Slice the bananas lengthways and drizzle the cut edges in honey. Warm the butter in a frying pan until foaming and fry the banana halves for 2 minutes until slightly softened. Carefully remove from the pan and arrange two halves on four flat plates, overlapping them slightly.

6. Take a warmed ice cream scoop and place a large scoop of the vanilla ice cream between the two banana slices on each plate. Then, scatter over the chopped peanut butter marshmallow pieces. Finally, top each banana split with a generous drizzle of both the chocolate and butterscotch sauces and an extra sprinkle of chopped peanuts.

Buttermilk Pancakes with Vanilla Mallows and Berry Compote

SERVES 4

125g (4½oz) plain flour
40g (1½oz) caster sugar
½ teaspoon bicarbonate of soda
½ teaspoon baking powder
Pinch of salt
350ml (12fl oz) buttermilk
1 large egg
50g (1¾oz) unsalted butter, melted
2 teaspoons vanilla bean paste
400g (14oz) mixed berries (fresh
  or frozen)
75g (2¾oz) caster sugar
4 Madagascan Vanilla Marshmallows
  (see page 14), cut into quarters
Oil and butter, for frying

The first time we tried buttermilk pancakes was when our friend Addison cooked us a traditional Canadian breakfast – they are similar to drop scones but the buttermilk gives them added sourness in flavour. The berry compote is super quick and easy to make and its sharp flavour works well with the sour pancakes and sweet marshmallows.

1. Combine the dry ingredients in a large bowl. In a separate bowl, whisk together the buttermilk, egg, melted butter and vanilla paste. Add the wet ingredients to the dry ingredients a tablespoon at a time, until you have a smooth thick batter. Set aside.

2. Put the mixed berries and sugar in a saucepan and gently warm over a medium heat until they start to break down and turn into a berry compote sauce – you may need to add a dash of water to loosen it slightly. Put a lid on the pan and set aside to keep warm.

3. Heat a heavy-based frying pan over a high heat. Oil the pan lightly and use a ladle to pour a ladleful of the pancake batter into the hot pan. Watch the pancakes; once you see the bubbles forming and popping on the surface it is time to flip them. The pancakes will be almost cooked so just need 30 seconds or so to finish them off on the other side before being put aside in a warm place while you make the rest.

4. Once all the pancakes are cooked, stack 2–3 pancakes on a plate, top with the vanilla marshmallow pieces, then gently pour hot berry compote over the top – the compote will run across the pancakes and the marshmallow will start to foam and melt.

Tip: The waffle toppings on page 131 are delicous as an alternative pancake topping.

Popcorn and Peanut Butter Marshmallow Bars

MAKES 10 BARS

150g (5½oz) chocolate-coated peanuts

30g (1⅛oz) unsalted butter

2 tablespoons smooth peanut butter

250g (9oz) Peanut Butter and Milk Chocolate Mallows *(see page 90)*, cut into small pieces, with the chocolate tops cut off – about 10 mallows

60g (2oz) plain popped popcorn

50g (1¾oz) chopped salted peanuts

23 x 23cm (9 x 9 inch) baking tin lightly sprayed with cake-release spray

These popcorn marshmallow bars can be made with any of our marshmallows – try the French Almond and Sour Cherry Mallows (see page 50), adding extra freeze-dried cherries and topping with crunchy flaked almonds.

1. Place the chocolate-coated peanuts in a freezer bag, seal and bash with a rolling pin. Set aside 50g (1¾oz) of them to be used as a topping.

2. Melt the butter in a small heavy-based saucepan over a medium heat. Turn the heat down to low and add the peanut butter and the marshmallows. Stir until smooth and then take the pan off the heat.

3. Add the popcorn, chopped salted peanuts and broken chocolate-coated peanuts to the peanut butter and marshmallow mixture. Use a spatula to stir everything together until fully combined.

4. Pour the mixture into the prepared tin, sprinkle over the reserved broken chocolate-coated peanuts and lightly press down with a spatula so they stick to the surface and a smooth layer is formed. Cover with cling film and chill in the fridge for 30 minutes.

5. Remove from the fridge and turn the set mixture out of the tin. Using a large sharp knife cut into 10 bars. They will keep for 2 days in an airtight container.

Triple Layer White, Milk and Dark Chocolate Marshmallows

MAKES 36 LARGE MARSHMALLOWS

For the white layer
1 medium egg white
60ml (2½fl oz) boiling water
12g (½oz) powdered gelatine
200g (7oz) white granulated
  or caster sugar
2 teaspoons golden syrup
100ml (3½fl oz) cold water
½ teaspoon vanilla bean paste

For the milk choc layer
1 large egg white
15g (½oz) powdered gelatine
75ml (2¾fl oz) boiling water
250g (9oz) white granulated
  or caster sugar
2 teaspoons golden syrup
100ml (3½fl oz) cold water
20g (¾oz) cocoa powder

For the dark choc layer
1 large egg white
15g (½oz) powdered gelatine
75ml (2¾fl oz) boiling water
250g (9oz) white granulated
  or caster sugar
2 teaspoons golden syrup
100ml (3½fl oz) cold water
50g (1¾oz) cocoa powder

To finish
Cornflour and icing sugar,
  for dusting
Cocoa powder

23 x 23cm (9 x 9 inch) baking
  tin lightly sprayed with cake-
  release spray

These marshmallows looks amazing with their three strata-like layers – perfect for a chocolate lover and a great addition to mallow pops and s'mores (see pages 78–87). We also use it in our Triple Chocolate and Brazil Nut Rocky Road on page 100.

1. First, make the white layer. Whisk the egg white using an electric stand mixer to stiff peaks and set aside. Pour the boiling water into a bowl, evenly sprinkle over the powdered gelatine and gently whisk until fully dissolved.

2. Use the sugar, golden syrup and cold water to make a hard-ball sugar syrup, add the gelatine and combine with the egg white until it turns glossy as described on page 10. Keep mixing on full speed for 5 minutes until the mixture is the same consistency as lightly whipped double cream. Add the vanilla paste in the last 30 seconds of mixing.

3. Pour the marshmallow into the baking tin. Make sure it is evenly spread out and cover with cling film. Set aside while you make the next layer.

4. Make the milk choc layer using the same method as the first layer, but add the cocoa powder at the end of mixing and fold in. Pour the milk choc mallow on top of the white layer. Make sure it is evenly spread, cover with cling film and set aside while you make the final layer.

5. Make the dark choc layer using the same method as the first layer, but add the larger quantity of cocoa powder at the end of mixing and fold in. Pour the dark choc layer on top of the milk choc layer. Make sure it is evenly spread out and cover with cling film. Leave to set as described on page 11.

6. Turn out and cut the mallow as described on page 11.

7. Enjoy these mallows straightaway as they are or keep in an airtight container for 2 weeks. Dust the tops of the mallows with cocoa powder to serve.

Triple Chocolate and Brazil Nut Rocky Road

MAKES 16 LARGE PIECES

225g (8oz) Triple Layer White, Milk and Dark Chocolate Marshmallows *(see page 98)* – about 9 pieces
Cornflour and icing sugar, for dusting
125g (4½oz) unsalted butter
3 tablespoons golden syrup
150g (5½oz) good-quality dark chocolate
150g (5½oz) good-quality milk chocolate
100g (3½oz) digestive biscuits, roughly crumbled up
100g (3½oz) roughly chopped brazil nuts
150g (5½oz) good-quality white chocolate

23 x 23cm (9 x 9 inch) baking tin lightly sprayed with cake-release spray
Piping bag fitted with a small nozzle

These indulgent chocolate rocky road biscuits are made with white, milk and dark chocolate, plus our triple chocolate marshmallows! The brazil nuts add a nutty crunch but could easily be omitted for more biscuits or another nut – macadamia or hazelnuts would work well.

1. Cut the mallows into 9 pieces lengthways so that all the layers can be seen (you will need plenty of cornflour and icing sugar for the cutting). Pop the mallows on a tray and into the freezer to chill.

2. Meanwhile, heat the butter, golden syrup and dark and milk chocolates in a heavy-based saucepan over a low heat until melted. Remove the pan from the heat.

3. Remove the mallows from the freezer. Stir half the marshmallow pieces, the roughly crumbled biscuits and chopped brazil nuts into the butter and chocolate mix.

4. Pour the mixture into the tin and use a spatula to press down into a smooth layer. Scatter the mixture with the remaining mallows, lightly pressing them into the surface of the rocky road mixture.

5. Cover with cling film and chill in the fridge for 2 hours. Remove from the fridge and lift the rocky road out of the tin. Use a large sharp knife to cut into 16 squares

6. Melt the white chocolate in a heatproof bowl over a pan of simmering water and spoon into a piping bag fitted with a small nozzle. Drizzle each piece of rocky road with the white chocolate. Leave the chocolate to set and then dust with icing sugar to serve. Rocky Road will keep for 5 days in an airtight container.

Lime and Dark Chocolate Marshmallow Teacakes

Teacake lovers rejoice – this super-tasty but sophisticated version ticks all the boxes when it comes to flavour.

MAKES 6

300g (10½oz) dark chocolate, chopped

For the biscuits
50g (1¾oz) wholemeal flour
50g (1¾oz) plain flour
Pinch of salt
½ teaspoon baking powder
25g (1oz) caster sugar
25g (1oz) unsalted butter
2 tablespoons semi skimmed milk

For the lime marshmallow filling
1 quantity of Marshmallow Crème
  (see page 17)
Juice of ½ lime
2 dashes of lime extract (optional)
¼ teaspoon natural green food
  colouring

7.5cm (3 inch) round cutter
Silicone mould for 6 teacakes
Piping bags with plain wide nozzle
  and small nozzle.

1. First make the biscuits. Put the flours, salt, baking powder and caster sugar in a bowl and rub in the butter with your fingertips until it resembles breadcrumbs. Add the milk and stir everything together to form a smooth ball.

2. On a floured work surface roll out the dough to about 4mm (⅛ inch) thick. Cut out 6 rounds with a 7.5cm (3 inch) round cutter and chill in the fridge for 10 minutes. Meanwhile, preheat the oven to 190°C/170°C fan/375°F/Gas Mark 5.

3. Transfer the chilled biscuits to a baking tray and bake for 10–12 minutes. When they're done, remove from the oven and leave to cool on a wire rack.

4. Next melt the chocolate. Put approximately 1 litre (35fl oz) water in a large saucepan and place a large heatproof bowl over the pan. Bring the water up to a steady simmer and then turn off the heat. Place 200g (7oz) of the chopped chocolate into the bowl and leave for 5–10 minutes, stirring occasionally, allowing the residual heat to melt the chocolate. Melting chocolate at a lower temperature results in a glossier finish.

5. Get your teacake mould and coat the inside of each mould with the melted chocolate – you'll need about 1 tablespoon of chocolate in each half-sphere. Use the back of a spoon to work the chocolate up and around the sides of the spheres, adding more chocolate if necessary. The chocolate needs to be thick enough to hold the shape of the teacake but not so thick that you end up with a chocolate-heavy teacake.

6. You should have some melted chocolate leftover. Take the cooled biscuits and dip one side in the remaining melted chocolate and set aside on a tray to harden.

7. Now, make the marshmallow filling – follow the Marshmallow Crème recipe on page 17. Once the crème is made, add the lime juice, lime extract and food colouring, mixing them in for 30 seconds. Spoon the mallow filling into a piping bag with a plain wide nozzle and pipe the mallow into each of the 6 chocolate-coated moulds, remembering to leave a 4mm (⅛ inch) gap at the top so the biscuit will sit flush. Carefully place the cooled biscuits on top of the mallow chocolate side down. The chocolate will stop the biscuit going soft.

8. Melt the remaining 100g (3½oz) chocolate and transfer into a piping bag with a small nozzle. Carefully pipe around circumference of the biscuit and pipe a small amount on top of each biscuit. Spread the chocolate evenly over the biscuit using a palette knife. Leave the teacakes to cool and set overnight or for at least 8 hours; do not refrigerate, as the chocolate will lose its glossy shine.

9. Carefully remove the teacakes from the moulds, trying not to handle them too much as fingerprints will mark the glossy dome. These teacakes will last for 2 days.

Raspberry and Coconut Marshmallow Biscuits

MAKES 18 BISCUITS

For the biscuits

50g (1¾oz) wheatgerm
50g (1¾ oz) wholemeal flour
50g (1¾oz) plain flour
1 teaspoon baking powder
50g (1¾oz) white caster sugar
50g (1¾oz) cold unsalted butter,
  cubed
30ml (1fl oz) buttermilk

For the topping

1 quantity of Marshmallow Fluff (see
  page 17) – follow the recipe, but
  use 16g (½oz) powdered gelatine
  and 10g (¼oz) freeze-dried
  raspberry powder
30g (1oz) organic desiccated
  coconut
75g (2¾oz) good-quality raspberry
  jam

These biscuits were a popular childhood treat for Ross, so he could not resist giving them the homemade treatment. We have kept the flavour combination classic but a great update would be vanilla mallow with strawberry jam or elderflower mallow with blackcurrant jam.

1. Take 4 sheets of greaseproof paper about 20 x 20cm (8 x 8 inches). In the centre of 3 of the sheets draw a 13 x 12cm (5 x 4½ inch) rectangle extending the lines to the edges of the paper to create a grid.

2. Sift the wheatgerm, both flours and the baking powder together in a large bowl and stir in the sugar. Rub the cubed cold butter into the flour and sugar mix with your fingertips until it looks like fine breadcrumbs. Add the buttermilk a teaspoon at a time, slowly mixing and bringing the dough together.

3. Divide the dough into 3. Roll one dough third between the 2 sheets of greaseproof paper, ensuring the bottom sheet has a pencil grid on it – the dough should be about 4mm (⅛ inch) thick.

4. Use a fluted pastry cutter to trim the excess dough away so the remaining dough is exactly 13 x 12cm (5 x 4½ inches) to match the rectangle on the paper. Divide the dough into 6 pieces, each measuring 6.5 x 4cm (2½ x 1½ inches).

5. Slide the paper covered in biscuits onto a flat baking tray and pop into the fridge to chill for 15 minutes. Repeat twice more with the remainder of the dough and the prepared greaseproof paper, until you have made at least 18 biscuits. Preheat the oven to 190°C/170°C fan/375°F/Gas Mark 5.

6. Remove the chilled biscuits from the fridge. Ensure there is a gap of about 3cm (1¼ inches) between each biscuit before baking in the oven for 6–8 minutes until just crisp. Leave to cool on a wire rack.

7. Make the Marshmallow Fluff as instructed on page 17 but increase the gelatine to 16g (½oz) and also mix in 10g (¼oz) freeze-dried raspberry powder. Spoon it into a piping bag fitted with a wide nozzle and pipe 2 beaded lines of the mallow fluff along the surface of each biscuit. Scatter the with the desiccated coconut.

8. Spoon the jam into a piping bag, snip a small hole and finish the biscuit by piping a line of jam down the middle. These biscuits are best eaten the day they are made.

Tip: if you want these biscuits to last longer, coat the surface with melted white chocolate before adding the topping – this will stop the biscuit from softening.

Salted Caramel and Dark Chocolate Mallows

MAKES 36 LARGE MARSHMALLOWS

2 medium egg whites
150ml (5fl oz) boiling water
32g (1¼oz) powdered gelatine
500g (1lb 2oz) white granulated
  or caster sugar
50ml (2fl oz) cold water
4 teaspoons golden syrup
1 teaspoon table salt
Cornflour and icing sugar,
  for dusting

For the topping

200g (7oz) good-quality dark
  chocolate, chopped
Maldon sea salt

23 x 23cm (9 x 9 inch) baking
  tin lightly sprayed with cake-
  release spray

These mallows have a slightly different technique to our other marshmallows. Other than a teaspoon of salt, no flavours or extracts are added – the sugar itself is made into a caramel to create the salted caramel flavour. It's a bit tricky but well worth it! These mallows are divine on hot chocolate or coffee or made into a s'more and the dark chocolate and sea salt topping finishes them off perfectly.

1. Whisk the egg whites using an electric stand mixer to stiff peaks and set aside. Pour the boiling water into a bowl, evenly sprinkle over the powdered gelatine and gently whisk until fully dissolved.

2. Sprinkle the sugar into a pan in an even layer. Set over a medium to high temperature and heat up the sugar in the pan, gently moving the pan in a circular motion to help it melt evenly – do not stir. Continue in this way until the sugar is a rusty brown colour and starts to smoke and small bubbles form. Take the pan off the heat, pour over the cold water and cover immediately with a lid. The water will evaporate almost instantly and will spit molten sugar, so you will need to act quickly.

3. Once the steam dies down, remove the lid and stir in the golden syrup and salt.

4. Add the gelatine and combine with the egg whites until they turn glossy as described on page 10. Keep mixing on full speed for 10 minutes until the mixture is the same consistency as lightly whipped double cream.

5. Pour the marshmallow into the baking tin, making sure it is evenly spread out, and cover with cling film. Leave to set as described on page 11.

6. Turn out and cut the mallow as described on page 11.

7. To make the chocolate topping, melt the chocolate as described on page 22 (step 6). Use a teaspoon to create a small disc of dark chocolate on the top surface of each mallow. Sprinkle a few crystals of sea salt in the centre of each chocolate disc and leave the chocolate to set before enjoying.

8. Enjoy these mallows straightaway or keep in an airtight container for 2 weeks.

Irish Coffee
Served with a Salted Caramel Mallow Stirrer

MAKES 4 CUPS

50g (1¾oz) dark chocolate
4 Salted Caramel Marshmallows
  (see page 106)
120ml (4fl oz) double cream
150ml (5fl oz) Irish whiskey
4-8 teaspoons brown sugar
800ml (27fl oz) freshly brewed
  hot espresso coffee

Wooden tea spoons
Irish coffee glasses

Making your marshmallows into stirrers is a great way to introduce your homemade treats to friends. Make the stirrers in advance so they are ready to use when after-dinner coffees are served.

1. First, make the marshmallow stirrers. Melt the dark chocolate in a heatproof bowl set over a pan of simmering water, making sure the bowl doesn't touch the water. Use a sharp knife to cut a small incision into the side edge of each marshmallow. Pour a small blob of the liquid chocolate onto the cut edge. Now insert a wooden spoon into each marshmallow, pushing the spoon through the chocolate into the cut. Set aside on greaseproof paper until the chocolate has set.

2. Lightly whisk the double cream and set aside. Warm the glasses by filling with hot water, discarding the water, then drying them ready to assemble the drink.

3. Add 1½ shots (75ml/2¾fl oz) of whiskey and 1–2 teaspoons sugar to each warmed glass. Top up each glass with the hot espresso coffee, leaving a space at the top. Gently stir, ensuring all the sugar dissolves.

4. Take a teaspoon and pour the lightly whisked cream over the back of the spoon into each glass, creating a generous cream layer over the coffee. Serve each glass with a salted caramel marshmallow stirrer on the side. As the marshmallow melts it will sweeten the coffee further and create a foamy layer.

Salted Caramel Chocolate Layer Cake

MAKES ONE LARGE CAKE (SERVES 16)

125ml (4fl oz) vegetable oil
350g (12oz) caster sugar
2 large eggs, beaten
225g (8oz) plain flour
85g (3oz) cocoa powder
1½ teaspoons baking powder
1½ teaspoons bicarbonate of soda
250ml (8½fl oz) milk
2 teaspoons vanilla extract
250ml (8½fl oz) boiling water

For the salted caramel marshmallow buttercrème

300g (11oz) granulated or caster sugar
50ml (2fl oz) cold water
½ teaspoon table salt
30g (1¼oz) golden syrup
3 medium egg whites
300g (10½oz) unsalted butter, softened
200g (7oz) icing sugar

For the praline decoration

100g (3½oz) sugar

Two 20cm (8 inch) springform cake tins lightly sprayed with cake-release spray
Piping bag fitted with a wide nozzle

This is the ultimate chocolate layer cake. We use oil instead of butter to give a super-soft springy sponge, which cuts really smoothly. Combined with the salted caramel marshmallow buttercrème, it's not to be messed with!

1. Preheat the oven to 200°C/180°C fan/400°F/Gas Mark 6. Line the greased cake tins with greaseproof paper and lightly spray the paper with more cake-release spray.

2. Use an electric stand mixer to beat all the cake ingredients together, except the boiling water, until you have a smooth, soft batter. Add the boiling water to the mixture a tablespoon at time, mixing constantly – the mixture will now be very liquid. Divide the mixture evenly between the 2 tins and bake for 25–35 minutes until the top is firm to the touch but springs back when lightly pressed with a finger. Remove from the oven and leave to cool completely in their tins.

3. Meanwhile, make the marshmallow buttercrème. Set a large heatproof bowl over a pan of simmering water. Put the sugar in a separate pan, with the water, salt and golden syrup and make a salted caramel following steps 2 and 3 from the Salted Caramel Marshmallow recipe on page 106. Once the caramel is ready, pour into the heatproof bowl and whisk with a handheld electric whisk, slowly adding the egg whites. Whisk for 12–14 minutes. Once the mixture forms stiff glossy peaks, cover and set aside.

4. Next, cream together the softened butter and icing sugar to make a buttercream. Add the buttercream to the salted caramel marshmallow crème a tablespoon at a time, beating in fully after each addition, until fully combined. Place the salted caramel marshmallow buttercrème in the fridge for 30 minutes to firm up.

5. To make the praline, make a caramel using the sugar and pour onto a baking sheet. Leave for 20 minutes to set.

6. To construct the cake, cut each cooled cake in half horizontally to give 4 layers. Place one layer of cake on a serving plate or stand. Transfer the marshmallow buttercrème to a piping bag fitted with a wide nozzle. Pipe a spiral of marshmallow buttercrème over the top of the first cake layer, leaving a 4mm (⅛ inch) gap around the edge. Gently take the next cake layer and place it on top of the buttercrème – under the weight of the next cake layer, the marshmallow buttercrème will spread slightly to the edge of the cake. Repeat with the remaining cake layers and marshmallow buttercrème until you have a 4-layer cake. To finish, pipe the marshmallow buttercrème over the top and smooth the surface with a palette knife. Crack the praline with a rolling pin and scatter over the top. Keep this cake in the fridge until ready to serve. The cake will keep for 3 days in the fridge.

Dark Chocolate, Jam and Marshmallow Biscuits

MAKES 12 LARGE BISCUITS

170g (6oz) unsalted butter, softened

160g (5¾oz) icing sugar

1 teaspoon vanilla bean paste

2 teaspoons runny honey

1 medium egg

335g (11½oz) plain flour

1 teaspoon baking powder

½ teaspoon bicarbonate of soda

200g (7oz) good-quality strawberry jam

1 quantity of Marshmallow Fluff (*see page 17*), but add ½ teaspoon vanilla extract

600g (1lb 6oz) good-quality dark chocolate, chopped

8cm (3¼ inch) round cutter

Piping bag fitted with a plain wide nozzle

These biscuits are nice and large – just as you remember them to be. We make them with strawberry jam, vanilla marshmallow and good-quality dark chocolate but feel free to get creative with other flavour combinations.

1. Beat the butter, sugar and vanilla together using an electric mixer for 5 minutes or until pale and fluffy. Scrape down the side of the bowl with a silicone spatula, add the honey and egg and beat until well combined. Scrape down again and add the flour, baking powder and bicarbonate of soda and beat on a low speed until well combined.

2. Divide the mixture into two and roll out each half in between 2 sheets of greaseproof paper until it is 5mm (¼ inch) thick. Lift off the top sheet of paper and use an 8cm (3¼ inch) biscuit cutter to cut out as many rounds as you can. Remove the dough trimmings, slide the paper covered in biscuits onto a flat baking tray and pop into the fridge to chill for 15 minutes. Repeat with the other half of the dough, and with all of the excess dough, until you have made at least 24 biscuits.

3. Preheat the oven to 200°C/180°C fan/400°F/Gas Mark 6. Remove the chilled biscuits from the fridge. Ensure there is a gap of at least 3cm (1¼ inches) between each biscuit before baking in the oven for 5–6 minutes until just golden. Leave to cool on a wire rack.

4. Once cooled, spread the underside of half the biscuits with some strawberry jam.

5. Make the Marshmallow Fluff as described on page 17, adding the vanilla extract for the final 30 seconds of mixing. Spoon into a piping bag fitted with a plain wide nozzle and pipe a spiral of mallow fluff on top of the jam layer. Top with another plain biscuit.

6. Melt 150g (5½oz) of the chocolate as described on page 22 (step 6). Use a palette knife to spread one side of the biscuit with the chocolate. Place on some greaseproof, then completely coat the top and sides with chocolate. Leave to cool again, and once set, enjoy. These biscuits will keep for 3 days.

Amaretto and Dark Chocolate Marshmallows

**MAKES 36 LARGE
MARSHMALLOWS**

2 medium egg whites
150ml (5fl oz) boiling water
30g (1⅛oz) powdered gelatine
500g (1lb 2oz) white granulated
  or caster sugar
4 teaspoons golden syrup
170ml (6fl oz) cold water
50ml (1¾fl oz) Amaretto liqueur
½ teaspoon almond extract
Cornflour and icing sugar, for
  dusting

For the topping
200g (7oz) good-quality dark
  chocolate, chopped
Crumbled hard Amaretti biscuits

23 x 23cm (9 x 9 inch) baking
  tin lightly sprayed with cake-
  release spray

Almondy and sweet with an amaretto kick, these mallows are a triple almond treat topped in dark chocolate and crumbled amaretti biscuits.

1. Whisk the egg whites using an electric stand mixer to stiff peaks and set aside. Pour the boiling water into a bowl, evenly sprinkle over the powdered gelatine and gently whisk until fully dissolved.

2. Use the sugar, golden syrup, cold water and 30ml (2 tablespoons) of the liqueur to make a hard-ball sugar syrup, add the gelatine and combine with the egg whites until they turn glossy as described on page 10. Keep mixing on full speed for 10 minutes until the mixture is the same consistency as lightly whipped double cream. Add the almond extract and remaining liqueur and mix for a further 30 seconds until completely mixed in.

3. Pour the marshmallow into the baking tin. Make sure it is evenly spread out and cover with cling film. Leave to set as described on page 11.

4. Turn out and cut the mallow as described on page 11.

5. For the topping, melt the milk chocolate as instructed on page 22 (step 6). Dip the top surface of each mallow into the melted chocolate and scatter with some crumbled amaretti biscuits. Leave the chocolate to set and enjoy.

6. Enjoy these mallows straightaway or keep in an airtight container for 2 weeks.

Serving suggestion Marshmallow Affogato

MAKES 4 CUPS

600ml (1 pint) freshly brewed hot
  espresso coffee
4 Amaretto Marshmallows (see
  above)
100ml (3½fl oz) Amaretto liqueur

An affogato is Amy's favourite way to finish an Italian meal as it combines, coffee, dessert and a liqueur all in one.

1. Warm 4 coffee cups (not espresso cups) by filling with hot water, discarding the water and then drying the cups ready to assemble the drink. Fill each warmed cup with hot coffee. Add the large marshmallow before topping with the shot of liqueur.

2. Alternatively, serve the coffee, marshmallow and liqueur in separate vessels to your guests and allow them to make their affogato themselves!

Espresso Coffee Mallows
Topped with Chopped Walnuts

MAKES 36 LARGE MARSHMALLOWS

2 medium egg whites
300ml (10½fl oz) hot, freshly made
  strong espresso coffee
30g (1⅛oz) powdered gelatine
500g (1lb 2oz) white granulated
  or caster sugar
4 teaspoons golden syrup
20g (¾oz) molasses
50g (1¾oz) chopped walnuts
Cornflour and icing sugar,
  for dusting

5 litre (9 pint) large heavy-based
  saucepan
23 x 23cm (9 x 9 inch) baking
  tin lightly sprayed with cake-
  release spray

This is one of our original recipes. These marshmallows are clearly inspired by the Soho coffee houses in London – made with real espresso and topped with chopped walnuts for that classic flavour combination.

1. Whisk the egg whites using an electric stand mixer to stiff peaks and set aside. Pour 100ml (3½fl oz) of the hot coffee into a bowl, evenly sprinkle over the powdered gelatine and gently whisk until fully dissolved.

2. Use the sugar, golden syrup, molasses and remaining coffee to make a hard-ball sugar syrup – use a large, high-sided, heavy-based saucepan of at least a 5 litre (9 pint) capacity as the mixture will bubble and spit as it comes to temperature – add the gelatine and combine with the egg whites until they turn glossy as described on page 10. Keep mixing on full speed for 10 minutes until the mixture is the same consistency as lightly whipped double cream.

3. Pour the marshmallow into the baking tin, making sure it is evenly spread out. Sprinkle the surface with chopped walnuts, then cover with cling film. Leave to set as described on page 11.

4. Turn out and cut the mallow as described on page 11.

5. Enjoy these mallows straightaway as they are or keep in an airtight container for 2 weeks.

Cocoa and Coffee Whoopee Pies

MAKES 12 LARGE
WHOOPEE PIES

For the cookies

225g (8oz) plain flour
100g (3½oz) good-quality cocoa
  powder, plus extra for dusting
1½ teaspoons bicarbonate of soda
½ teaspoon Maldon sea salt
75g (2¾oz) unsalted butter,
  softened
100g (3½oz) granulated sugar
110g (3¾oz) soft light brown sugar
1 medium egg
235ml (8fl oz) semi-skimmed milk
1 teaspoon vanilla bean paste

For the coffee filling

1 quantity of Marshmallow Crème
  (see page 17)
100g (3½oz) icing sugar
150g (5½oz) unsalted butter
2 teaspoons strong instant coffee
  dissolved in 1 teaspoon of hot
  water

A classic cocoa and coffee combination, these massive whoopee pies are an absolute joy to eat!

1. Preheat the oven to 200°C/180°C fan/400°F/Gas Mark 6. Sift together the flour, cocoa powder, bicarbonate of soda and salt into a medium bowl and set aside.

2. Place the butter and both sugars into the bowl of an electric stand mixer fitted with a paddle attachment and mix on a high speed for about 3 minutes until smooth. Add the egg and mix for a further 2 minutes until pale and fluffy.

3. Mix in half the flour mixture until smooth. Add the milk and vanilla paste and mix again until loose and smooth. Add the remaining flour and mix for a further minute until completely combined.

4. Line 2 large baking trays with greaseproof paper. Drop 2 teaspoons of the dough for each cookie onto the baking trays, spacing them apart by about 8cm (3¼ inches) – you should fit about 6 on each tray. Bake for 12–14 minutes or until the cookies spring back when lightly touched. Transfer from the baking sheets to wire racks and leave to cool. Repeat with the remaining mixture to make 12 more cookies.

5. To make the coffee filling, make the Marshmallow Crème as instructed on page 17 and set aside. Cream together the icing sugar and butter using an electric stand mixer. Once smooth and fluffy, add the coffee and mix until completely combined. Beat in the Marshmallow Crème.

6. Transfer the coffee mallow filling into a piping bag fitted with a wide nozzle. Assemble the whoopee pies by sandwiching two cookies together with plenty of coffee mallow filling in the middle. Dust with cocoa powder to serve.

Ale Marshmallows
Topped with Milk Chocolate Pretzels

MAKES 36 LARGE MARSHMALLOWS

2 medium egg whites
300ml (10fl oz) ale or full-bodied beer, whisked to release some of the bubbles
30g (1⅛oz) powdered gelatine
500g (1lb 2oz) white granulated or caster sugar
50ml (2fl oz) cold water
4 teaspoons golden syrup
30g (1¼oz) molasses
Cornflour and icing sugar, for dusting

For the topping

200g (7oz) good-quality milk chocolate, chopped
36 chocolate-coated mini pretzels

5 litre (9 pint) heavy-based saucepan
23 x 23cm (9 x 9 inch) baking tin lightly sprayed with cake-release spray

The ale in these marshmallows gives a subtle malty flavour. Topped in milk chocolate and slightly salted chocolate-covered mini pretzels they are a fun treat for a beer lover!

1. Whisk the egg whites using an electric stand mixer to stiff peaks and set aside.

2. Pour 150ml (5fl oz) of the ale into a heavy-based saucepan and bring to the boil. Take off the heat, evenly sprinkle over the powdered gelatine and gently stir in with a whisk until fully dissolved.

3. Use the sugar, remaining ale, cold water, golden syrup and molasses to make a hard-ball sugar syrup – use a large, high-sided, heavy-based saucepan of at least a 5 litre (9 pint) capacity as the mixture will bubble and spit as it comes to temperature – add the gelatine and combine with the egg whites until they turn glossy as described on page 10. Keep mixing on full speed for 10 minutes until the mixture has the same consistency as lightly whipped double cream.

4. Pour the marshmallow into the baking tin. Make sure it is evenly spread out and cover with cling film. Leave to set as described on page 11.

5. Turn out and cut the mallow as described on page 11.

6. To make the topping, melt the chocolate as instructed on page 22 (step 6). Dip the top surface of each mallow in the melted chocolate and then top each mallow with a single chocolate-coated pretzel. Leave the chocolate to set, then enjoy!

7. Enjoy these mallows straightaway or keep in an airtight container for 2 weeks.

CHAPTER SIX

FESTIVE TREATS

American Peppermint Mallows

**MAKES 36 LARGE
MARSHMALLOWS**

2 large egg whites
150ml (5fl oz) boiling water
30g (1⅛oz) powdered gelatine
500g (1lb 2oz) white granulated
  or caster sugar
4 teaspoons golden syrup
200ml (7fl oz) water
1 teaspoon American peppermint
  extract
½ teaspoon natural green food
  colouring
Cornflour and icing sugar, for
  dusting

23 x 23cm (9 x 9 inch) baking
  tin lightly sprayed with cake-
  release spray

These minty marshmallows pep up whatever you pair with them and work perfectly with hot chocolate.

1. Whisk the egg whites to stiff peaks using an electric stand mixer and set aside. Pour the boiling water into a bowl, evenly sprinkle over the powdered gelatine and gently stir in with a whisk until fully dissolved.

2. Use the sugar, golden syrup and water to make a hard-ball sugar syrup, add the gelatine and combine with the egg whites until they turn glossy as described on page 10. Keep mixing on full speed for 10 minutes until the mixture is the same consistency as lightly whipped double cream. Add the peppermint extract and food colouring and mix for a final 30 seconds.

3. Pour the marshmallow into the baking tin, making sure it is evenly spread, then cover with cling film. Leave to set as described on page 11.

4. Turn out and cut the mallow as described on page 11.

5. Enjoy these mallows straightaway as they are or keep in an airtight container for 2 weeks.

Tip: To make shaped mallows, split the mixture between two baking trays to create thinner layers of mallow, then you can use biscuit cutters – we like little stars – to cut out the shaped mallow floats.

Hot Chocolate with Mint Mallow Floats

MAKES 4 MUGS

70g (2½oz) dark (minimum 70% cocoa
  solids) chocolate
35g (1¼oz) milk chocolate
1.2 litres (2 pints) semi-skimmed milk

¼ teaspoon ground cinnamon
2 tablespoons icing sugar
3 tablespoons cocoa powder
Pinch of sea salt
4 American Peppermint Mallows
  (see opposite)

1. For the hot chocolate, finely chop all the chocolate and then warm
the milk in a large pan over a medium heat until almost boiling.

2. Once the milk is bubbling remove from the heat and add the chocolate
pieces. Stir with a whisk until the chocolate has melted into the milk.

3. Then, add the rest of the ingredients and stir gently with the whisk until you
have a nice smooth consistency. You can set aside now, if you like, and reheat
when the mallow is ready; it will need to be hot enough to melt the mallow.

4. When ready to serve, place a mallow on top of the hot chocolate and enjoy!

Candy Cane Marshmallow Brownies

MAKES 12 BROWNIES

115g (4oz) unsalted butter

200g (7oz) good-quality dark chocolate, roughly chopped

150g (5½oz) granulated sugar

50g (1¾oz) soft light brown sugar

1 teaspoon vanilla bean paste

3 large eggs

80g (3oz) plain flour

30g (1oz) cocoa powder

Pinch of salt

1 quantity of Marshmallow Fluff (*see page 17*)

¼ teaspoon American peppermint extract

½ teaspoon natural red food colouring

Red and white candy canes, to decorate

Two 23 x 23cm (9 x 9 inch) baking tins lightly sprayed with cake-release spray

These lovely little brownies have a soft layer of peppermint marshmallow running through them. To echo the crunchy candy cane topping we make this mallow marbled red and white.

1. Melt the butter and roughly chopped chocolate in a small heavy-based saucepan set over a medium heat. Stir constantly for about 5 minutes until fully melted and set aside to cool for 10 minutes.

2. Preheat the oven to 200°C/180°C fan/400°F/Gas Mark 6. Line the greased baking tins with greaseproof paper, leaving the edges of the paper hanging over the side. Lightly spray the paper with more cake-release spray.

3. Use a balloon whisk to mix the sugars and vanilla paste into the chocolate and butter mixture. Next, whisk in the eggs, one at a time. Fold in the flour, cocoa powder and pinch of salt and mix until fully combined.

4. Pour the brownie mixture evenly into the two prepared baking tins. Bake in the oven for 12 minutes or until the brownies just start to pull away from the edge of the tin. Allow the tins to cool and then pop one in the fridge to chill.

5. Make the Marshmallow Fluff as described on page 17, adding the peppermint extract about 30 seconds before you finish whisking. Fold in the red food colouring gently so it is marbled throughout the fluff. Pour the peppermint fluff over the left out tin of brownie. Remove the chilled brownie from the fridge and gently lift it out of the tin, placing it carefully on top of the marshmallow layer in the other tin. Put the marshmallow and brownie sandwich back in the fridge for 2 hours to fully firm up.

6. When fully set, remove the tin from the fridge, carefully lift the brownie sandwich out of the tin and use a long sharp knife to cut it into 12 even squares. Roughly chop up two red and white candy canes and scatter the shards over the brownies to serve. They will keep for 3 days in an airtight container.

Green Apple and Cinnamon Mallows
with a Cashew Crumb

MAKES 36 LARGE MARSHMALLOWS

2 medium egg whites
90ml (3fl oz) boiling water
36g (1½oz) powdered gelatine
½ teaspoon ground cinnamon, plus extra for dusting
500g (1lb 2oz) white granulated or caster sugar
4 teaspoons golden syrup
225ml (8fl oz) apple purée
50ml (2fl oz) cold water
1 teaspoon natural green food colouring
Cornflour and icing sugar, for dusting

For the cashew crumb

25g (1oz) unsalted butter
25g (1oz) ground salted cashew nuts
75g (2¾oz) chopped salted cashew nuts
25g (1oz) light soft brown sugar

23 x 23cm (9 x 9 inch) baking tin lightly sprayed with cake-release spray

Delicious green apple purée makes these mallows flavoursome and combined with cinnamon, is a true taste of autumn. The cashew crumb topping is slightly salted, giving that apple crumble texture and taste.

1. First, make the cashew crumb. Preheat the oven to 200°C/180°C fan/400°F/Gas Mark 6. Melt the butter in a heavy-based saucepan over a low heat and stir in the ground and chopped cashews and brown sugar. Spoon the mixture into a baking tray and spread into an even layer. Bake in the oven for 15 minutes, stirring halfway through. Set aside to cool until needed.

2. Now, make the marshmallow. Whisk the egg whites using an electric stand mixer to stiff peaks and set aside. Pour the boiling water into a bowl, evenly sprinkle over the powdered gelatine and cinnamon and gently whisk until fully dissolved.

3. Use the sugar, golden syrup, cold water and 150ml (5fl oz) of the apple purée to make a hard-ball sugar syrup, add the gelatine and combine with the egg whites until they turn glossy as described on page 10. Keep mixing on full speed for 5 minutes, stop the mixer and add the remaining apple purée. Turn the mixer back on to full speed for a further 5 minutes until the mixture is the same consistency as lightly whipped double cream. Add the green food colouring and mix for another 30 seconds until completely mixed in.

4. Pour the marshmallow into the baking tin, making sure it is evenly spread out. Sprinkle the surface with cashew crumb and a little extra ground cinnamon, then cover with cling film. Leave to set as described on page 11.

5. Turn out and cut the mallow as described on page 11.

6. Enjoy these mallows straightaway as they are or keep in an airtight container for 2 weeks.

Waffles and Streaky Bacon Served with Apple and Cinnamon Mallows

SERVES 4

12 smoked streaky bacon rashers
8 small or 4 large waffles
(homemade or shop-bought)
4 large Green Apple and Cinnamon
Mallows *(see page 128)*
Maple syrup, to drizzle

This is a real holiday breakfast treat – hot fresh waffles served with salty, crispy smoked streaky bacon, green apple marshmallows and an extra drizzle of maple syrup. The bacon really brings out the apple flavour of the mallows and as they melt they create a foamy sweet sauce with the syrup – delicious!

1. Grill or griddle the smoked streaky bacon until crispy. Meanwhile, make or toast your waffles and keep them warm on a plate in the oven.

2. Slice the mallows into smaller triangular wedges.

3. Once ready to serve, stack 3 slices of bacon over the waffles on each plate and top with a handful of the mallows – they will immediately start to melt. Drizzle with a splash of maple syrup and enjoy!

Waffles Topped with Braised Apples and Apple and Cinnamon Mallows

SERVES 4

25g (1oz) butter
2 large eating apples, peeled, cored
and roughly sliced
25g (1oz) caster sugar
8 small or 4 large waffles
(homemade or shop-bought)
4 large Green Apple and Cinnamon
Marshmallows *(see page 128)*,
sliced into smaller rectangular
pieces
Ground cinnamon, to serve

If bacon and marshmallows doesn't take your fancy, try this recipe instead – the butter-braised apples are very easy to make and deliciously warming. The topping also works well on the Buttermilk Pancakes on page 94.

1. Melt the butter in a saucepan over a gentle heat. Add the sliced apples and sugar and slowly cook down until you have a chunky braised apple sauce. Set aside and keep warm.

2. Make or toast your waffles. Once ready to serve; arrange the waffles across 4 plates, top with a generous spoonful of the braised apples and a handful of the mallows – they will immediately start to melt. Dust with some ground cinnamon to serve.

Caramallows

These dark chocolate marshmallow caramels can be made with any of our mallows. Serve them alongside the Chocolate Marshmallow Cups (see opposite) as petits fours.

MAKES 36 CARAMALLOWS

3 large marshmallows (flavour of your choice)
Cornflour and icing sugar, for dusting
115g (4oz) unsalted butter
120ml (4¼fl oz) double cream
250g (9oz) granulated sugar
30g (1oz) golden syrup
3 tablespoons cold water
350g (12oz) good-quality dark chocolate, chopped
Maldon sea salt, to garnish

23 x 23cm (9 x 9 inch) baking tin lightly sprayed with cake-release spray

1. Line the greased baking tin with greaseproof paper, leaving the edges of the paper hanging over the side. Lightly spray the paper more with cake-release spray. Cut the marshmallows into 16 pieces each, giving you 48 small pieces. Dust with the cornflour and icing sugar mix, transfer to a container and pop in the freezer.

2. Melt the butter and double cream in a small heavy-based saucepan set over a medium heat. Once fully melted, take off the heat and set aside.

3. Use the sugar, golden syrup and cold water to make a sugar syrup, just as you would when making the marshmallows (see page 10) but heat the syrup until 160°C (320°F). Once it has come to temperature, take off the heat and slowly add the butter and cream mixture – watch out the sugar will foam up! Put the mixture back over the heat and cook until the temperature reaches 115°C (239°F), stir and then pour it into the prepared baking tin. Set aside for 4 hours to allow the caramel to cool.

4. Use the overhanging greaseproof paper to lift the caramel out of the tin and onto a flat chopping board. Pop in the fridge for 30 minutes to firm up. Remove the chopping board from the fridge and use a sharp knife to cut the caramel into 36 squares.

5. Remove the marshmallows from the freezer and place a piece in the centre of each caramel square. Bring the corners of the caramel together around the piece of mallow, gently seal up the edges and mould into a rough ball. Place the caramels onto a flat baking sheet lined with greaseproof paper, press down slightly to flatten them and then pop them in the fridge for 20 minutes to firm up.

6. Melt 250g (9oz) of the chocolate as described on page 22 (step 6). Take each caramel and drop them into the chocolate one at a time, using a fork to make sure they are fully coated. Place the caramels back on the baking sheet and run the fork gently over the top to create grooves. Sprinkle with sea salt and and leave to set at room temperature for about 4 hours. The caramels will last for 1 week stored in an airtight container.

Marshmallow Chocolate Cups

These bite-sized cups can be made all year round with any flavour marshmallow and any type of chocolate. Here we've made them using milk chocolate with peanut butter and lemon marshmallows. These tiny treats are perfect as little stocking fillers.

MAKES 48 SMALL CUPS

350g (12oz) good-quality milk chocolate
3 Lemon and Poppy Seed Marshmallows *(see page 30)*
3 Peanut Butter Marshmallows *(see page 90)*
Cornflour and icing sugar, for dusting

48 small fairy cake cases

1. Arrange the fairy cake cases on a tray. Melt 250g (9oz) of the chocolate as instructed on page 22 (step 6). Use a teaspoon to spoon a small amount of melted chocolate into the bottom of each fairy cake case – just enough to cover the bottom of the case. Set aside the cake cases, leaving the chocolate to set slightly. The remaining chocolate should stay workable for 15–20 minutes.

2. Cut all the marshmallows into 8 pieces, giving you a total of 24 small pieces for each flavour. Dust with the cornflour and icing sugar mix, transfer to a container and pop in the freezer for 10 minutes to firm up.

3. Remove the marshmallows from the freezer and place on top of the slightly set chocolate in each fairy cake case. Use a teaspoon to top up the cases with the remaining melted chocolate, covering the mallow completely.

4. Leave the chocolates for about 4 hours at room temperature to set. If you can't wait that long, place the chocolates in the fridge for 30 minutes but just be aware the chocolate may discolour a little. Once set and hard to touch, take the trays out of the fridge and remove the paper cake cases, revealing the chevron edge of the chocolate cups. The chocolate cups will last for 2 weeks stored in an airtight container.

Spiced Gingerbread Marshmallows

MAKES 36 LARGE MARSHMALLOWS

2 large egg whites
150ml (5fl oz) boiling water
30g (1⅛oz) powdered gelatine
2 cloves
1½ teaspoons ground ginger
1 teaspoon ground cinnamon
500g (1lb 2oz) white granulated
    or caster sugar
4 teaspoons golden syrup
30g (1⅛oz) molasses
200ml (7fl oz) cold water
Cornflour and icing sugar, for
    dusting

For the topping

50g (1¾oz) crystallized stem ginger,
    cut into slices
100g (3½oz) good-quality dark
    (minimum 70% cocoa solids)
    chocolate, melted

5 litre (9 pint) heavy-based
    saucepan
23 x 23cm (9 x 9 inch) baking
    tin lightly sprayed with cake-
    release spray

These spiced gingerbread mallows are topped with a slice of fiery crystallized ginger dipped in dark chocolate – perfect for any festive gathering.

1. Whisk the egg whites to stiff peaks using an electric stand mixer and set aside. Pour the boiling water into a bowl, evenly sprinkle over the powdered gelatine and gently stir in with a whisk until fully dissolved.

2. Grind the cloves to a fine powder in a pestle and mortar and mix with the ground ginger and cinnamon. Add the spices to the gelatine and water mix.

3. Use the sugar, golden syrup, molasses and cold water to make a hard-ball sugar syrup – use a large, high-sided, heavy-based saucepan of at least a 5 litre (9 pint) capacity as the mixture will bubble and spit as it comes to temperature – add the gelatine and combine with the egg whites until they turn glossy as described on page 11. Keep mixing on full speed for 5–10 minutes until the mixture has the same consistency as lightly whipped double cream.

4. Pour the marshmallow into the baking tin, making sure it is evenly spread and then cover with cling film. Leave to set as described on page 11.

5. Turn out and cut the mallow as described on page 11. Dip the slices of crystallized ginger into the melted chocolate and carefully place on top of each cut marshmallow.

6. Enjoy these mallows straightaway or keep in an airtight container for 2 weeks.

Gingerbread Loaf Cake
with a Marshmallow Buttercrème Frosting

This gingerbread loaf cake is warming and spicy and the thick layer of sweet gingerbread marshmallow buttercrème heightens its festive flavours. Serve a generous slice on a crisp December afternoon with a cup of hot tea.

SERVES 12

175g (6oz) unsalted butter, softened
175g (6oz) dark muscovado sugar
45g (1½oz) molasses
45g (1½oz) golden syrup
265g (9½oz) plain flour
3½ teaspoons ground ginger
1 teaspoon ground cinnamon
¼ teaspoon ground clove
¼ teaspoon ground allspice
2 medium eggs, beaten
3 pieces of stem ginger from a jar
  of sugar syrup, finely chopped
200ml (7fl oz) milk
1 teaspoon bicarbonate of soda
2 pieces of crystalized ginger,
  chopped, to decorate

For the marshmallow buttercrème topping

⅔ quantity of Marshmallow Crème (*see page 17*) plus the following ingredients:
  1 tablespoon molasses
  ½ teaspoon ground ginger
  ¼ teaspoon ground cinnamon
  ⅛ teaspoon ground allspice
100g (3½oz) unsalted butter,
  softened
65g (2¼oz) icing sugar

23 x 13cm (9 x 5 inch), 900g (2lb) loaf tin, lightly sprayed with cake release spray and lined with greaseproof paper
Piping bag fitted with a wide nozzle

1. Preheat the oven to 180°C/160°C fan/350°F/Gas Mark 4. Melt the butter, sugar, molasses and golden syrup in a small heavy-based saucepan set over a medium heat. Stir constantly for about 5 minutes until fully melted and smooth and then set aside to cool slightly.

2. Put the flour and spices in a large bowl, add the butter and sugar mixture and stir to combine. Stir in the eggs and chopped ginger.

3. Warm the milk gently in a pan, add the bicarbonate of soda – it will foam up a little and then add it to the gingerbread mixture. Stir until fully mixed in and smooth.

4. Pour the mixture into the prepared loaf tin and bake for 45 minutes until the top is firm to the touch but springs back when lightly pressed with a finger. Remove from the oven and leave to cool completely in the tin.

5. Meanwhile, make the Marshmallow Crème as described on page 17, reducing the ingredients and mixing times by one-third, and add the molasses with the golden syrup and the spices at the end, 30 seconds before you finish whisking. Once finished cover and set aside.

6. Cream together the butter and icing sugar to make a buttercream, then beat this into the gingerbread marshmallow crème, a tablespoon at a time, until fully combined.

7. Remove the cooled loaf cake from its tin. Transfer the gingerbread marshmallow buttercrème topping to a piping bag fitted with a wide nozzle and carefully pipe a smooth zig zag of crème across the top of the loaf cake. Sprinkle with the chopped crystallized ginger to decorate. The cake will keep for 3 days.

Clove, Clementine and White Choc Mallows

MAKES 36 LARGE MARSHMALLOWS

2 medium egg whites
90ml (3fl oz) boiling water
36g (1¼oz) powdered gelatine
⅛ teaspoon ground cloves
500g (1lb 2oz) white granulated or caster sugar
4 teaspoons golden syrup
280ml (9fl oz) fresh clementine juice (about 8–10 fruits)
1 teaspoon orange extract
Grated zest of 12 clementines
200g (7oz) good-quality white chocolate, chopped
Cornflour and icing sugar, for dusting

23 x 23cm (9 x 9 inch) baking tin lightly sprayed with cake-release spray

Clementines and cloves have a really distinctive festive flavour. Topping with white (or dark) chocolate and freshly grated clementine zest gives a decadent finish. Bag these up as an alternative Christmas gift.

1. Whisk the egg whites to stiff peaks using an electric stand mixer and set aside. Pour the boiling water into a bowl, evenly sprinkle over the powdered gelatine and gently whisk until fully dissolved. Add the ground cloves.

2. Use the sugar, golden syrup and 150ml (5fl oz) of the clementine juice to make a hard-ball sugar syrup and add the gelatine as described on page 10. Once all the bubbles have dissipated, add the remaining clementine juice.

3. Turn the electric mixer to a medium speed and add the sugar syrup to the egg whites as described on page 10. Keep mixing on full speed for 10 minutes, until the mixture is the same consistency as lightly whipped double cream. Add the orange extract and zest of the clementines used for juicing and mix for a further 30 seconds until completely mixed in.

4. Turn off the mixer and pour the marshmallow into the baking tin, making sure it is evenly spread, then cover with cling film. Leave to set as described on page 11.

5. Turn out and cut the mallow as described on page 11.

6. Now you're ready to decorate. Melt the chocolate as described on page 22 (step 6). Dip the top of each mallow in the melted chocolate, then freshly zest the remaining clementines over the wet chocolate so they are scattered with zest. Leave to set.

7. Enjoy these mallows straightaway or keep in an airtight container for 2 weeks.

Eggnog with Clementine Marshmallow Stirrer

MAKES 8 GLASSES

50g (1¾oz) good-quality white chocolate, chopped

8 Clove, Clementine and White Chocolate Marshmallows (see page 138)

700ml (1¼ pints) semi-skimmed milk

300ml (10fl oz) double cream

3 cinnamon sticks

1 teaspoon vanilla extract paste

1 teaspoon grated nutmeg

5 large egg yolks

100g (3½oz) granulated sugar

8 shots (200ml/7fl oz) Bourbon whiskey

8 wooden teaspoons

8 glasses/cups

We first made eggnog when we were at university hosting Christmas dinner in our halls of residence – it's rather a novelty and anything boozy goes down well with students! Our Clementine mallow stirrers zing it up a bit and make it particularly festive.

1. First, prepare your clementine stirrers. Melt the white chocolate in heatproof bowl set over a pan of simmering water (making sure the bowl doesn't touch the water). Use a sharp knife to cut a small incision into the side edge of each marshmallow. Pour a small blob of the liquid chocolate onto the cut edge. Insert a wooden teaspoon into the marshmallow, pushing it through the chocolate into the cut. Put aside until the chocolate has set and secured the mallow in place.

2. Gently heat the milk and cream in a small heavy-based saucepan over a medium heat. Once simmering, add the cinnamon sticks, vanilla paste and nutmeg, take off the heat and set aside to steep.

3. In an electric stand mixer, cream together the egg yolks and sugar until fully combined and thick and runny. Turn down to slow and add in the warm milk mixture, a ladleful at a time until all the mixture is combined and smooth. Stir in the Bourbon. At this point the mixture can be refrigerated for up to 3 days.

4. Transfer the smooth mixture into a large heatproof bowl set over a pan of gently simmering water (making sure the bowl doesn't touch the water). Bring the mixture back up to warm temperature while gently stirring it. When ready to serve, pour the mixture into 8 glasses or cups and submerge a mallow stirrer in each glass.

Sweet Potato Cake
with Vanilla Mallow Topping

SERVES 12

700g (1½lb) sweet potatoes (about 2-3 medium sized potatoes)
115g (4oz) unsalted butter, softened
190g (6½oz) soft light brown sugar
250g (9oz) plain flour
1¾ teaspoons baking powder
½ teaspoon bicarbonate of soda
½ teaspoon table salt
1 teaspoon ground cinnamon
1 teaspoon ground ginger
⅛ teaspoon ground cloves
2 medium eggs
½ teaspoon vanilla extract

For the topping

1 quantity of Marshmallow Crème
  (*see page 17*)
½ teaspoon vanilla bean paste

20cm (8 inch) springform cake tin

This cake is a great alternative to carrot cake – the sweet potatoes add sweetness and moisture and the marshmallow topping looks incredible. It is very easy to make so it's well worth putting a bit more effort into the piped marshmallow topping to give it the wow factor.

1. Prick the surface of the sweet potatoes with a knife. Place in a bowl, cover and microwave on full power for 10–15 minutes until the flesh is cooked through and soft. Set aside to cool.

2. Preheat the oven to 200°C/180°C fan/400°F/Gas Mark 6. Grease and line the cake tin with greaseproof paper. Remove the skin of the cooled cooked potatoes and mash the flesh until smooth. Set 350g (12oz) of the mashed potato aside.

3. In a large bowl, beat the butter and sugar together in an electric stand mixer for 2–3 minutes until light and fluffy. Next sift all of the remaining dry ingredients together in a bowl.

4. Add the eggs and vanilla to the sugar and butter mix and beat until combined. Add the 350g (12oz) of the mashed sweet potato and mix in thoroughly. Finally fold in the mixed dry ingredients and stir until a fully combined cake mixture. Pour into the prepared tin and bake for 35–40 minutes until cooked. Leave to cool on a wire rack.

5. Once cooled, remove from the tin and place in the centre of the platter or stand you want to serve it on. Make the Marshmallow Crème, adding the vanilla paste 30 seconds before the end, and transfer into a piping bag fitted with a wide nozzle. Squeeze out about a tablespoons worth of the crème onto the cake and use a palette knife to spread over the cake in a thin layer. Then starting in the centre, pipe large droplets of marshmallow crème onto the surface of the cake, working in concentric circles until it is fully iced.

6. The topping will lose its glossy finish over time, so it's best to pipe this as close to serving as possible. This uniced cake will keep for 3 days if stored in a cake tin.

Maple and Cinnamon Marshmallows
with Pecan Praline and Cranberries

MAKES 36 LARGE MARSHMALLOWS

2 medium egg whites
140ml (3fl oz) boiling water
30g (1⅛oz) powdered gelatine
500g (1lb 2oz) white granulated or caster sugar
4 teaspoons golden syrup
200ml (7fl oz) cold water
100ml (3½fl oz) maple syrup
½ teaspoon ground cinnamon
75g (2¾oz) Pecan Praline (see page 18), chopped
25g (1oz) freeze-dried sliced cranberries (air-dried cranberries can also be used)
Cornflour and icing sugar, for dusting

23 x 23cm (9 x 9 inch) baking tin lightly sprayed with cake-release spray

These marshmallows have a real complexity of flavours and textures. Maple syrup and cinnamon are traditionally paired together but combining them with sweet and salty crunchy pecan praline and sour chewy cranberries gives it a more grown-up twist.

1. Whisk the egg whites to stiff peaks using an electric stand mixer and set aside. Pour the boiling water into a bowl, evenly sprinkle over the powdered gelatine and gently whisk until fully dissolved.

2. Use the sugar, golden syrup and cold water to make a hard-ball sugar syrup, add the gelatine and combine with the egg whites as described on page 10. Add the maple syrup and cinnamon and keep mixing on full speed for 10 minutes, until the mixture is the same consistency as lightly whipped double cream.

3. Turn off the mixer and pour half the marshmallow mixture into the baking tin. Gently sprinkle over the chopped pecan praline, then add the remaining marshmallow mixture on top. Make sure the mixture is evenly spread before scattering with a layer of the freeze-dried cranberries. Cover with cling film and leave to set as described on page 11.

4. Turn out and cut the mallow as described on page 11.

5. Enjoy these mallows straightaway or keep in an airtight container for 2 weeks.

Sweet 'Jacket' Potatoes
with Molten Vanilla Marshmallows

SERVES 6

3 large sweet potatoes
Salt
Freshly ground black pepper
Butter
6 Madagascan Vanilla Marshmallows
  (see page 14)
Cornflour and icing sugar,
  for dusting

Sweet potato pie with marshmallow topping is a popular holiday treat in the States. We've twisted the traditional recipe for this simple take on a Brit classic – jacket potatoes. The resulting dish is sweet with crispy, sticky skins and goes surprising well with roast chicken or pulled pork.

1. Preheat the oven to 220°C/200°C fan/425°F/Gas Mark 7. Wash and dry the sweet potatoes and stab all over with a fork. Place the sweet potatoes on a baking tray in the oven and bake for 1 hour, turning halfway through.

2. Remove the potatoes from the oven and cut them in half, scraping out the flesh into a separate bowl. Pop the skins back in the oven for 5–10 minutes to crisp up more. Meanwhile, mash the sweet potato flesh with a little butter, salt and pepper to taste.

3. Cut up the marshmallows into small chunks, dusting them with the cornflour and icing sugar.

4. Take the potato skins back out of the oven and fill them with the mashed sweet potato. Top each potato with a sprinkling of the marshmallow chunks. Place the potatoes under a very hot grill to caramelize the surface of the marshmallows – or if you have one use a kitchen blowtorch.

Morello Cherry and Kirsch Marshmallows

These marshmallows were inspired by Amy's favourite chocolate cherry liqueurs. They have a triple cherry hit – made with both morello cherry purée and cherry kirsch liqueur. We then like to top ours with a chocolate-dipped maraschino cherry – use the ones with stalks for added drama!

**MAKES 36
LARGE MARSHMALLOWS**

2 medium egg whites
90ml (3fl oz) boiling water
36g (1¼oz) powdered gelatine
500g (1lb 2oz) white granulated
    or caster sugar
4 teaspoons golden syrup
50ml (2fl oz) cold water
225ml (8fl oz) cherry purée
40ml (1½fl oz) Kirsch
Cornflour and icing sugar, for
    dusting

For the topping

250g (9oz) good-quality dark
    chocolate, chopped
36 maraschino cherries (with stalks)

23 x 23cm (9 x 9 inch) baking tin
    lightly sprayed with cake-release
    spray

1. Whisk the egg whites using an electric stand mixer to stiff peaks and set aside. Pour the boiling water into a bowl, evenly sprinkle over the powdered gelatine and gently whisk until fully dissolved.

2. Use the sugar, golden syrup, cold water and 150ml (5½fl oz) of the cherry purée and 25ml (1fl oz) of the Kirsch to make a hard-ball sugar syrup, add the gelatine and combine with the egg whites until they turn glossy as described on page 10. Keep mixing on full speed for 5 minutes, stop the mixer and add the remaining cherry purée. Turn the mixer back on to full speed for a further 5 minutes until the mixture is the same consistency as lightly whipped double cream. Add the remaining kirsch and mix for another 30 seconds until completely mixed in.

3. Pour the marshmallow into the baking tin. Make sure it is evenly spread out, then cover with cling film. Leave to set as described on page 11.

4. Turn out and cut the mallow as described on page 11.

5. To make the topping, melt the chocolate as described on page 22 (step 6). Carefully use a spoon to create a small circular blob of melted chocolate on top of each cut mallow. Hold the cherries by their stalks and dip each one into the remaining melted chocolate so that they are half covered. Gently rest them on top of the chocolate disc on the mallow. Leave to set before enjoying.

6. Enjoy these mallows straightaway or keep in an airtight container for 2 days.

Flavour variation # Pear and Brandy Marshmallows

Make as above but substitute the cherry purée and Kirsch for the same amount of pear purée and brandy. You may also want to add 1 teaspoon natural green food colouring to the mallow mixture 30 seconds before you turn off the mixer. Top with melted dark chocolate and broken brandy snaps.

Chocolate and Cherry Kirsch Cupcakes

MAKES 12 CUPCAKES

200g (7oz) fresh or frozen cherries
175g (6oz) granulated sugar
1 tablespoon Kirsch
125g (4½oz) unsalted butter,
  softened
100g (3½oz) good-quality dark
  chocolate, roughly chopped
50g (1¾oz) light muscovado sugar
Pinch of salt
2 large eggs, beaten
150g (5½oz) self-raising flour

**For the marshmallow buttercrème
topping**

1 quantity of Marshmallow Crème
  (see page 17)
150g (5½oz) unsalted butter,
  softened
100g (3½oz) icing sugar
¼ teaspoon natural pink food
  colouring
⅛ teaspoon natural blue food
  colouring
15g (½oz) freeze-dried cherry
  powder
1 tablespoon Kirsch

12-hole cupcake tin and cupcake
  cases
Piping bag fitted with a wide nozzle

These dark chocolate cupcakes are made with homemade cherry compote in the batter. They look great topped with our purple Kirsch marshmallow buttercrème frosting.

1. First, make the cherry compote. Warm the cherries (if you are using fresh cherries, you will need to de-stone them first) with 75g (2¾oz) of the granulated sugar and the kirsch in a small heavy-based saucepan over a medium heat. Stew for 10 minutes until the fruit starts to break down and has reduced by a third. Take off the heat and set aside to cool. Preheat the oven to 200°C/180°C fan/400°F/Gas Mark 6 and line the cupcake tin with the cases.

2. Melt the butter and roughly chopped chocolate in a small heavy-based saucepan over a medium heat. Stir constantly for about 5 minutes until fully melted and then set aside to cool for 10 minutes.

3. Stir in the cherry compote, remaining granulated sugar, muscovado sugar, salt and eggs. Add the flour and keep stirring until fully combined.

4. Spoon the mixture evenly into the 12 cupcake cases, then bake for 25 minutes. Leave the cupcakes to cool on a wire rack.

5. Meanwhile, make the topping. Make the Marshmallow Crème (see page 17), cover and set aside. Cream together the softened butter and icing sugar to make a buttercream, adding the food colouring, cherry powder and Kirsch at the end. Add the buttercream to the Marshmallow Crème a tablespoon at a time until fully combined.

6. Transfer the purple marshmallow buttercrème to a piping bag fitted with a wide nozzle. Carefully pipe a swirl of the topping on top of each cupcake and top with a cherry to finish, if liked. These cupcakes will keep for 2 days.

Marshmallow Baubles

MAKES 12–16 BAUBLES

1 quantity of Spiced Gingerbread
  Marshmallows (*see page 134*)
200g (7oz) dark chocolate
Edible metallic cake decorations
  (optional)
Cornflour and icing sugar,
  for dusting

Two 23 x 23cm (9 x 9 inch) baking
  tins lightly sprayed with cake-
  release spray
Christmas shape cookie cutters
Piping bag fitted with a fine nozzle
Small cellophane bags or packets
Ribbon

These marshmallow baubles are really fun to make and any of the festive flavours in this chapter would work well. Make a combination of 3 or 4 flavours a few days before Christmas and give them as gifts to houseguests, pop them on the tree or save some for stocking fillers!

1. Make a quantity of Spiced Gingerbread Marshmallows (see page 134) but split the mixture across two tins to give 2 thin layers about 1.5cm (¾ inch) thick. Once set, turn the layers out onto a surface dusted with the cornflour and icing sugar mix.

2. Use the Christmas shape cookie cutters to cut out shapes from the marshmallows, gently dusting each shape with the cornflour and icing sugar mix as you go. You will need to wash the cutters between using each one to make sure you get a clean cut. Each tin of mallow should yield 6–8 shapes. The leftover marshmallow is great chopped up and used to top hot chocolate.

3. Take all the shapes and dust as much of the cornflour and icing sugar off as possible. Melt the chocolate as described on page 22 (step 6). Transfer the melted chocolate to a piping bag fitted with a very fine nozzle. Carefully pipe simple designs or messages onto the mallow shapes. Sprinkle some of the wet chocolate with edible metallic decorations, if you wish. Set aside for the chocolate to set.

4. Once set, carefully slide the shapes into cellophane bags and seal the bags with a ribbon. The bags can now be hung on the tree as an alternative to shop-bought chocolate decorations, attached to gifts or used as stocking fillers. The baubles will keep for up to 2 weeks.

Mallow Mince Pies

MAKES 24

225g (8oz) plain flour, plus extra
 for dusting
60g (2oz) icing sugar
1 egg yolk
1 tablespoon ice-cold water
1 teaspoon lemon juice
140g (5oz) salted butter, at room
 temperature
450g (1lb) jar of good-quality
 mincemeat

For the topping
1 quantity of Marshmallow Crème
 (see page 17)
1 tablespoon molasses
½ teaspoon ground ginger
¼ teaspoon ground cinnamon
⅛ teaspoon allspice

7.5cm (3 inch) round cutter
24-hole pastry tin
Piping bag fitted with a wide nozzle

Homemade mince pies are delicious, and these versions are even better with their gingerbread marshmallow topping. Serve to guests at Christmas-time and they'll never touch a shop-bought mince pie again!

1. First, make the pastry. Sift the flour and icing sugar together in a bowl. Put the egg yolk, water and lemon juice in a small bowl and mix together with a fork.

2. Put half the flour and sugar mixture in a large mixing bowl. Cut the butter into the bowl of flour and sugar, drawing a knife through until the butter and flour is lightly mixed together. Add the egg yolk mixture and mix with a fork until well combined.

3. Add the rest of the flour and sugar mixture and bring together into a smooth ball. Knead gently on a floured surface until smooth. Wrap in cling film and leave to rest in a cool place for 1 hour.

4. Divide the pastry in half and roll each half out on a floured surface. Cut out 12 discs from each half using a 7.5cm (3 inch) round cutter. Place each disc into the holes of a pastry tin.

5. Preheat the oven to 200°C/180°C fan/400°F/gas mark 6. Put a teaspoon of the mincemeat in each pie and crimp the edges. Bake in the oven for 20–25 minutes until golden. Remove from the oven and leave to cool on a wire rack.

6. Meanwhile, make the Marshmallow Crème following the instructions on page 17, but add the molasses with the golden syrup and add the spices in the last 30 seconds before you finish whisking. Transfer the gingerbread crème to a piping bag fitted with a wide nozzle and carefully pipe a swirl on top of each of the cooled mince pies to finish. Over time, the topping will lose its glossy finish, so it's best to pipe this as close to serving as possible. The mince pies will keep for 2 days in an airtight container.

USEFUL INFORMATION

Egg whites

Use fresh free-range or organic egg whites. Our medium egg whites are 35g (1¼oz) and a large egg white is 40g (1½oz). Alternatively, use pasteurized free-range liquid egg white – available from most supermarkets.

We recommend: Two Chicks (UK & Ireland); All Whites (USA); Puregg (Australia).

Fruit purée

You can make your own (see page 19) or buy ready-made purée – Ella's Kitchen Smoothie Fruits (technically baby food) are organic and available from all supermarkets. Or Funkin Cocktails Funkin Pro Cocktail Purées are all 100 percent natural and come in a wide range of flavours.

We recommend: Ella's Kitchen, Funkin Cocktails (UK & Ireland); Plum Organics (USA); Mamia (Australia).

Freezing

Marshmallows freeze incredibly well! Make them, pop them in an airtight container and put them straight in the freezer. You can keep them in the freezer for up to 4 weeks. They defrost quickly in just twenty minutes and are as fresh as you just made them.

Freeze-dried fruit powder

Fruit powders are a useful way of adding real fruit and natural colour to marshmallow mixes. We get ours from healthysupplies.co.uk and msk-ingredients.com – they also sell freeze-dried sliced strawberries, cherries and cranberries.

We recommend: Healthy Supplies (UK & Ireland); MSK Ingredients (Worldwide).

Gelatine

We use powdered beef gelatine (we find powdered gelatine more accurate to measure for our recipes than leaf gelatine). There are many brands you can use such as Dr. Oetker (available in all supermarkets), Great Lakes Kosher Gelatine and Chef William. Gelatine is incredibly good for you, it's good for your gut health, your joints, skin and hair – we can't recommend it enough!

We recommend: Dr. Oetker, Chef William (UK & Ireland); Great Lakes (USA & Australia).

Gelatine alternatives

Gelatine alternatives such as carrageenan can be used to set marshmallow and jellies. Carrageenan is not digestible so has no nutritional value and there is research that links

it to intestinal problems. It is not available everywhere but if avoiding gelatine is important to you, you should be able to order it from specialist baking suppliers.

We recommend: Sous Chef (UK & Ireland); Modernist Pantry (Worldwide).

Natural food colour, extracts and essences

If possible we colour and flavour our mallows with the natural fruits and nuts used in the recipe. Sometimes we want to heighten the colour or flavour so we use natural food colours, real extracts and natural essences. Synthetic colours and flavours trigger migranes for some people so we keep things all natural. We use some supermarket own-brand natural colours and many natural colours from PME (available in baking shops and online). For extracts and essences we use Nielsen Massey and Uncle Roy also both widely available in baking shops and online.

We recommend: PME, Nielsen Massey, Uncle Roy (UK & Ireland); Hopper Natural Colours, Premium Gourmet Food (Australia); Americolor, Culinary Crystals, Nature's Flavours (USA).

Nut butter

We use Whole Earth smooth peanut butter, which is 96% peanuts and 4% vegetable oil. For other nut butters either purchase as natural as possible or make your own with 100g (3½oz) toasted nuts blended with 2 tablespoons vegetable oil and a pinch of salt – easy and delicious!

We recommend: Whole Earth (UK & Ireland); Smucker's (USA); Sanitarium (Australia)

Packaging

To keep your marshmallows soft and fresh for longer always package them in airtight clip-lid food storage boxes – we use 'Clean and Click' available from Lakeland. Alternatively they can be stored in clip-top glass jars such as Kilner, Dunelm or Le Parfait. For brightly coloured mallows we recommend popping a piece of greaseproof paper between each layer of mallow to prevent the colours from bleeding into each other.

INDEX

ACKNOWLEDGEMENTS

Firstly thank you to all our friends and family, who have supported us over the past two years and listened to us talk about marshmallows constantly! We hope that the many samples we have treated you to somewhat makes up for putting up with us! Particular thanks to Julie, Graham, Jon, Jenny, Harry, Maddy, Sally, Bobby, Charlotte, Michael and Ann (The Nelsons) and Geraldine, Dermot Aoiffe, Youseff, Afrah, Eoghan and Sam (The O'Briens) and our good friends Cesca, Simon, Olivia, Sebastian, Addison, Jamie, Natalie and Justin.

In order of our short history, thank you to Adam, Alex, Rachel, Steve and Mark for trying our mallows at the Slaughtered Lamb and to all of Ross' ex-colleagues who dug deep and bought our mallows at that first Christmas fair – you all gave us the confidence to give it a go!

Also special thanks again to Eoghan for designing our much-loved logo and to Sian and Stacey for all those ad-hoc design jobs Amy sprung on you! And thanks again to Alex for shooting our mallows that gloomy December day so we could get our website up and running. Lucy and Olly – thank you for letting us loose at your wedding and Annette and Adam for believing in a local brand.

To all the wonderful traders we have met on the way at Old Spitalfields Market, Newington Green Farmers market and of course Broadway Market – we thank you and think of you all often.

Massive thanks to Emily at T & Shop – our first stockist and wholesale partner. Also thanks to both notonthehighstreet.com and yumbles.com for inviting us to trade on your sites – you opened our eyes to eCommerce!

Thank you to our agents Diane and Robyn for pushing us to write this book and the team at Jacqui Small (Jacqui, Fritha, Rachel, Abi, Cynthia and Keiko) for believing in us and making it all happen (and patiently teaching us along the way).

Finally, thank you to everyone and anyone who has bought one of our mallows – this is all down to you!